Administration of
Government Documents Collections

Administration of Government Documents Collections

Rebekah M. Harleston
and
Carla J. Stoffle

Libraries Unlimited, Inc., Littleton, Colo.

1974

Library of Congress Card Number 74-81960
International Standard Book Number 0-87287-086-3

LIBRARIES UNLIMITED, INC.
P.O. Box 263
Littleton, Colorado 80120

Table of Contents

Introduction

In any library collection, a manual of the processing procedures for library materials is acknowledged to be an asset, whether as a training aid for new staff members or as a refresher for administrators. *Administration of Government Documents Collections* is a manual of the procedures involved in processing government documents, in libraries with either separate or integrated collections of federal documents.

Because of the diversified nature of a government documents collection, it can be viewed as a microcosm of the library as a whole. Thus, the objective of this handbook is to cover all major aspects of both technical and public services for government documents collections. Chapters are designed to: 1) introduce or explain the necessity for the routines described; 2) enumerate the specific steps at each stage of processing; and 3) present the exceptions and problems incurred at each stage with appropriate methods for handling.

A brief overview of government publishing and the depository system is provided in chapter one. Chapter two explains the principles of the Superintendent of Documents classification system and discusses the advantages and disadvantages of using it. Bibliographic control is introduced in chapter three, while subsequent chapters discuss types and forms of records, acquisitions sources and procedures (receiving requests, executing orders, etc.), and details for handling the day-to-day routines. These routines include both the basic (e.g., sorting the mail, filing, shelving) and the specialized (e.g., searching for entries and classification numbers, handling changes made by the Superintendent of Documents, transferring or reclassifying documents). Throughout this volume, many illustrations of cards, forms, and records are included to enhance the usefulness of the text.

Based on the authors' experience and advice from many documents librarians, this handbook will not explore *all* the alternatives practiced in every library. However, the procedures described represent efficient methods for library handling of federal documents. Thus, this manual can provide a useful basis for improving and evaluating existing procedures.

Since Ellen Jackson's *A Manual for the Administration of the Federal Documents Collection in Libraries* was published nearly twenty years ago, many changes have occurred. Significant reorganization in the government and a great increase in specialization have resulted in an increase in the volume of government publications and a broader scope of materials. *Administration of Government Documents Collections* provides comprehensive, up-to-date information for handling library problems that have resulted from these changes. It is well organized, easy to use, and thoroughly indexed.

Chapter 1

HISTORY AND DEVELOPMENT OF GOVERNMENT PUBLISHING AND DEPOSITORY SYSTEMS

The evolution of definitions of U.S. government documents or government publications follows the changes in the nature and scope of federal publishing activities. The early term commonly used for government documents and government publications was "public documents." The official definition of public documents was approved by the 29th Congress in 1847 as "those publications or books that have been or may be published, procured or purchased by order of either House of Congress or by joint resolution of the Houses"; by 1874, the definition was changed to mean all publications printed by order of both or either House.[1]

The Joint Committee on Printing, which serves as a sort of board of directors for the Government Printing Office, defined the terms "document" and "publication" in this way in the Regulations of 1949:

> The term "publication" as used in these regulations shall be construed to mean any printed matter of which there is a free public distribution, but shall not include laws, rules, regulations, instructions, opinions, decisions, and official notices and circulars required for official use by officers of the Government.
>
> The term "document" as used in these regulations shall be construed as applying to forms and publications such as pamphlets and books, and to such publications as are expressly designated to be documents, of which there is a free public distribution.[2]

More recently, Public Law 90-620, which enacted Title 44, United States Code, "Public Printing and Documents," put forth the following definition in Chapter 19, "Depository Library System": "Government publication as used in this chapter, means informational matter which is published as an individual document at Government expense, or as required by law."[3]

A more precise definition, found in the *Checklist of United States Public Documents, 1789-1909*, is the one that is generally accepted. It states:

> Any publication printed at Government expense or published by authority of Congress or any Government publishing office, or of which an edition has been bought by Congress or any Government office for division among members of Congress or distribution to Government officials or to the public, shall be considered a public document.[4]

Because of the changes in modern technology, the word "processed" has been incorporated into the above.

Prior to 1860, private printers were contracted to print government material, but this led to many difficulties. Each area of government could select its own publisher, and frequently information that was essentially the same, with only minor differences, was published by two or three agencies. For example, some House and Senate documents were almost identical and appeared as departmental publications with only minimal alterations. Another problem caused by this method was the lack of continuity of printers. Often, whenever the congressional balance of power shifted, a new printer was hired, regardless of his qualifications. Knowing that his appointment was not permanent, the printer turned out as many contracts as possible, often overlooking such time-consuming details as accuracy, editing, completeness, etc. The result was a hodge-podge of facts, statistics, and information that, in some instances, bore little resemblance to previous documents except in subject matter.

The Government Printing Office was created by Congressional Joint Resolution 25, on June 23, 1860. At first, it was limited to publishing congressional materials, but in time it took on the printing and binding work of the governmental units. The Public Documents Division, headed by the Superintendent of Documents, was set up as a division of the GPO; most of the task of distributing official publications was centralized in this office. A simple system of classifying publications by the issuing office was devised, and depository libraries were established. However, there was not yet any concerted effort either to organize the publications program or to maintain copies of what had been printed. Neither was there any medium for intelligent distribution.

Before the establishment of designated depositories or any other systematic method for distribution of government publications, special acts of Congress were passed at various times to provide for the printing of enough copies of the Senate and House public journals for distribution to executives and legislatures of the states and territories. Provision was made, also sporadically, to supply documents to colleges, universities, and historical societies. On December 27, 1813, however, a resolution was passed to provide that copies of the public journals and documents of that and every succeeding Congress should be sent to every college, university, and historical society in the United States. This same resolution authorized the printing of 200 copies in addition to the usual number.

Subsequent resolutions increased both the number of copies printed and the types of publications. A resolution of January 28, 1857, as amended by the resolution of March 20, 1858, was the real foundation for the depository library network that exists today. This network is a cooperative program between the federal government and designated major libraries throughout the United States. Under this program certain classes of government publications are supplied free to those libraries, for the purpose of making such publications readily accessible to the general public.

Section Three of the 1857 resolution stated:

> And be it further resolved, That the Journals and Congressional
> documents heretofore deposited in the Library of Congress, by authority
> of the above cited resolutions, and so many of the four hundred copies
> of the public documents sent to the Department of State as are now
> distributed by the Department to colleges and other literary institu-
> tions, shall be deposited with the Secretary of Interior, for distribu-
> tion to such colleges, public libraries, athenaeums, literary and
> scientific institutions, boards of trade, or public associations as may
> be designated by him.[5]

The following year the resolution was amended by striking out the words "by him"
and inserting the words, "to him by the Representatives in Congress from each
Congressional district and by the delegates from each territory in the United
States."[6]

Thus the act of 1857 and its amendment removed the distribution responsibility from the Department of State and gave it to the Office of the Secretary of
the Interior; and it gave the Congressman the power to designate depositories.

A further amendment to the 1857 resolution was passed on February 5,
1859. A portion of this act provided that each Senator could designate a library; it
also directed that distribution should be made first to those states not yet covered
by distribution and that from then on the distribution should be kept equal in each
congressional district and territory. This act also established the official library for
all public documents and the position of Superintendent of Documents.[7]

The General Printing Act of 1895 was the next significant legislation concerning government printing and distribution of documents. Although it has been somewhat changed, it can still be termed the underlying structure of the depository
library system. By provisions of the Act, the distributing of publications, formerly
a function of the Department of the Interior, and the duties of the Superintendent
of Documents became a responsibility of the Government Printing Office. Designation of depositories remained essentially as established by the amended 1857 law
except for a provision regarding investigation of depositories by the Superintendent
of Documents. With the exception of a few important amendments (e.g., in 1922
the law was revised to allow depository libraries to select the material they wished
to receive) there were no major revisions of the depository library laws from 1895
to 1962.

For a period of time, identifying a document was relatively simple. The
Government Printing Office did the major portion of producing the literature. But
with the proliferation of government agencies, the explosion of knowledge, and
the decentralization of the federal government, subsidiary printing plants were
authorized. The law that permitted distribution of materials printed at the Government Printing Office was fairly satisfactory as long as the GPO was able to handle
most of the government's printing. The subsidiary presses, however, tended to place
an arbitrary limitation on the availability of those non-GPO publications through
the depository system. By 1962 the Public Printer reported that there were 352
such government presses that were not under his control.

The Depository Library Act of 1962 corrected this problem by providing that
all government publications except those printed for official use or those of a

classified nature were to be made available for public information to depository libraries, through the facilities of the Superintendent of Documents. As Schmeckebier and Eastin pointed out in 1969, "This is a program with tremendous problems of administration and coordination."[8] The results of those "tremendous problems" may now be becoming evident in the recent GPO announcements of price increases ranging from 100 to 1000 percent and new procedures for handling standing orders.

Another significant feature of the Depository Library Act of 1962 is the provision for an increased number of depositories. Under the provision of the 1895 law, a single depository library for each congressional district was to be designated by the representative; an additional two depositories were permitted for each state, to be designated by each Senator of the state. In 1962, there were 594 actual depositories out of a possible total of 720, with some states having several vacancies. Under the 1962 Act, the possible number of depositories increased to 1,350, permitting a total of two depositories for each congressional district and two for each Senator.

Another provision of the 1962 Act established a system of regional depository libraries, making it possible for two regional depositories to be selected from the existing depositories in each state. These regional depositories must accept and retain all government publications made available to depositories, and must agree to provide interlibrary loan, reference service, and assistance to the regular depositories in the disposition of unwanted government publications. The provision for disposition permits those libraries that are serviced by regional depositories to dispose of publications that they have retained for at least five years. The regional depository may offer the disposed publications to other depositories within the area, then to other libraries. If the publications are not wanted by any of these, then they may be discarded. This procedure does much to simplify the almost impossible discarding policy of the past.

The law currently in force is Public Law 90-620 (44 USC), which states: "That the general and permanent laws relating to public printing and documents are revised, codified, and enacted as Title 44 of the United States Code 'Public Printing and Documents'." Under this law the possible total number of depository libraries is 1,390. However, some of the 1,110 currently existing depositories are outside the scope of this theoretical total of 1,390. This is so because in several instances there are three or more depository libraries in the same congressional district, all designated by representatives, due to redistricting after a decennial census.

In addition to defining depository libraries, the law also sets forth requirements for the physical appearance of the book and enumerates the kinds of reports to be made by the several departments and agencies of the government.

Chapter 19, "Depository Library Program," gives detailed information and instructions concerning the kinds of libraries that may become depository, the conditions under which they must operate, and reasons for losing depository status. Section 1902 of that chapter determines the kinds of publications that shall be available through the Superintendent of Documents:

> Government publications, except those determined by their issuing components to be required for official use only or for strictly administrative or operational purposes which have no public interest or

educational value and publications classified for reasons of national security. . . .[9]

Libraries may be designated as depositories in any of the following ways:

1. By the U.S. Representative of a congressional district;

2. By a state's U.S. Senator;

3. By virtue of being a state library or a land-grant college library;

4. By special act of Congress;

5. By being the highest appellate court in a state;

6. By being an executive department, service academy, and independent agency.[10]

TYPES OF GOVERNMENT PUBLICATIONS

Acquisitions problems, procedures, and sources are discussed in detail in Chapter 4. This section is an introduction to the types of materials available from the federal government.

Federal government publications are divided into three broad classes: 1) executive publications; 2) legislative or congressional publications; and 3) judicial documents, corresponding roughly to the three coordinate branches of the government.

Executive publications are those published by the several executive departments or independent agencies. To acquire a working knowledge of the changing governmental structure, it is essential to use the *United States Government Manual* and many other guides that will be discussed later. There are thousands of serial and monographic publications of the executive branch, ranging from extremely specialized to very popular treatments. The following examples indicate their scope: 1) presidential papers, including every communication to Congress. Most of these are printed as documents of Congress. In addition, public papers of the President of the United States are published annually, covering one calendar year, while proclamations and executive orders are published in separate sets. 2) Departmental publications—e.g., publications of the State Department (treaties, executive agreements, diplomatic correspondence, *Department of State Bulletin*, *Foreign Policy Briefs*, directories of diplomatic and consular service, etc.). 3) Publications of independent agencies—e.g., the General Services Administration (includes the National Archives), the General Accounting Office, or Atomic Energy Commission.

Congressional publications include materials published under the authority of Congress as a whole, of either House, or of any committee of either House.[11] There are the following types of materials: debates and proceedings; hearings; legislation, including bills, laws, statutes, and codes; and reference works, including miscellaneous publications. Congressional debates have been reported in *Annals of the Congress*, 1st Congress to the end of the 1st session of the 18th Congress,

1789-1824; *Register of Debates*, 2d session of the 18th Congress to end of 1st session of the 25th Congress, 1824-37; *Congressional Globe*, 1st session of the 23d Congress to end of the 42d Congress, 1833-73; *Congressional Record*, 1st session of the 43d Congress to the present, 1873 to date. *Congressional Record* is published in three forms: the daily record, the paperbound bi-weekly record, and the permanent bound record printed in several parts. For each session of Congress, a *House Journal* and *Senate Journal* is published, and each volume of both journals is indexed separately, both by subject matter and by bill number. Legislative matters usually proceed through investigating committees, which hold hearings and gather data to support legislative actions. Reports of congressional committees are published in a House and Senate Report series. The Senate and House Documents series cover a variety of material, mainly reports of special investigating committees. Combined with the House and Senate Reports, most of the collection is variously known as "Congressional set," "Serial set," or "Congressional series." Selected reprints of publications of the first 14 Congresses, 1789-1816, were gathered together and reprinted under the title *American State Papers*.

Judicial publications comprise several groups, including publications of several courts—for example, the Supreme Court, Circuit Courts of Appeals, District Courts, Court of Claims, Customs Court, etc. The published laws of the United States fall into three well-defined groups:[12] 1) series embracing all the laws printed in chronological order; 2) codifications of all the permanent and general laws in force; and 3) compilations dealing with laws on particular services or subjects. In the slip-law edition, each act is published separately as soon as it is enacted, and these slip-laws are divided into two series—public and private—which are separately numbered. At the end of any session of Congress, all of the laws of that session are published in the final and permanent form in the *Statutes at Large*. Beginning with Volume 52 (1938), each volume contains the laws enacted by one Congress. About every five years the *United States Code* is published, being a collection of all general and permanent laws in force. The first edition of the *United States Code* was published in 1926 under the title *The Code of the Laws of the United States . . . of a General and Permanent Character in Force December 7, 1925, and Appendix with Laws to December 6, 1926. . . .* Cumulative supplements to the *United States Code* are issued after each session of Congress. Since 1926 there have been six editions, the last one (*United States Code, 1970 Edition*) containing consolidation and codification of all the general and permanent laws in force on January 20, 1971.

The three types of documents discussed above—executive publications, congressional publications, and judicial publications—are relatively easy to identify and obtain. There are others, however, which are often difficult to identify and/or obtain. In the past, material has been compiled by an arm of the government and published either directly by a government press or by a specified commercial publisher. Today's publishing program is, to say the least, less easily categorized. Among the types of publications that cause difficulties are 1) interdepartmental publications; 2) publications arising from government contracts or grants; 3) publications from regional government presses; and 4) publications from quasi-governmental bodies.

Interdepartmental publications are not always published and distributed by the agency that initiated the research. This fact compounds the difficulty of assigning the author of the piece, and it frequently complicates the acquisition process.

Contracts and grants account for a great deal of the research and study presently being accomplished. In such cases the author pursues his own path, from his subject and method of presentation to his choice of how the material will finally appear. Thus, work prepared under contract or grant may be published as a book, a dissertation, a journal article, or one of a continuing and established series. It may not even appear in printed form, in fact, but as film or some medium other than the printed page. *Government Reports Announcements* and *Government Reports Index*, *Research in Education*, *STAR*, and *Nuclear Science Abstracts* are only a few of the major governmental indexing and abstracting services that may be used as sources of information about the publication program in a given field. These and other sources are discussed in Chapter 3.

Regional government presses compound the difficulties mentioned above. Agencies are turning more and more frequently to regional governmental presses, which do not necessarily report to the Superintendent of Documents, or to private presses, which almost never forward a copy to the Superintendent of Documents Library to be cataloged.

Quasi-governmental bodies are often operated to some degree by private donations or foundations. To the extent that their programs are financed by such funding, there is frequently a lack of communication between the agency and the Superintendent. These programs, such as some of the Smithsonian Institution and its component parts, the National Science Foundation and the National Academy of Science, are only partially governmental, and the publications stemming from them often appear as trade or society titles.

These two difficulties—of identifying and acquiring—are inherent in the nature of documents and are met in a variety of ways. There are many avenues to follow when acquiring and administering a documents collection. These begin with a patron's request or a bibliographical citation and end when the document is shelved in the library's collection. Methods, bibliographic sources, procedures, and acquisitions sources are enumerated in the following chapters.

FOOTNOTES

[1] William L. Post, "Centralization: A Needed Reform in Public Document Distribution," *Library Journal* 34:43 (February 1909).

[2] U.S. Congress. House. Committee on House Administration. Subcommittee to Study Federal Printing and Paperwork. *Paperwork Management and Printing Facilities in the United States Government.* Part II, House Report No. 2945 (Washington, Government Printing Office, 1956), p. 2.

[3] 82 Stat. 1238 (1968), 44 U.S.C. 1901.

[4] U.S. Documents Office, *Checklist of United States Public Documents, 1789-1909.* 3d ed. rev. and enl. (Washington, Government Printing Office, 1911), p. vii.

[5] *The Congressional Globe*; Appendix, 34th Congress, 3d Session, January 28, 1857, p. 429.

[6] *Ibid.*, 35th Congress, 1st Session, March 20, 1858, p. 583.

[7] 11 Stat. 379.

[8] Laurence F. Schmeckebier and Roy B. Eastin, *Government Publications and Their Use,* 2d ed. (Washington, Brookings Institution, 1969), p. 129.

[9] 82 Stat. 1238 (1968), 44 U.S.C. 1902.

[10] U.S. Congress. Joint Committee on Printing, *Government Depository Libraries: The Present Law Governing Designated Depository Libraries*, rev. (Washington, Government Printing Office, 1973), pp. 1-2.

[11] Schmeckebier and Eastin, *op. cit.*, p. 119.

[12] *Ibid.*, p. 189.

Chapter 2

SUPERINTENDENT OF DOCUMENTS
CATALOGING AND CLASSIFICATION

The Superintendent of Documents Classification System was created in the Library of the Division of Public Documents sometime between 1895 and 1903, when the classification of U.S. documents was begun. At that time, it was decided that this scheme would follow the principle of archival arrangement rather than subject arrangement and would use the distinguishing word of the title of all governmental establishments as the first word of all main entries.[1]

The first explanation of the scheme was provided by William Leander Post in the preface to a *List of Publications of the Agriculture Department, 1862-1902.* Post gave credit for the development of the classification scheme, which is essentially classification by government author, to Adelaide R. Hasse, who used it as the basis for assigning classification numbers to Department of Agriculture publications from 1841 to 1895.[2]

Like any other classification scheme used over a period of time, this one has expanded and refined its details of methods and use. The basis of the present scheme is the grouping together of the publications of the departments, agencies, bureaus, etc., according to the organizational structure of the government with subordinate agencies and offices grouped under the parent organization.

The main points of the classification scheme, as represented in the *Monthly Catalog*, were finally settled while the third edition of the *Checklist* was being compiled. At this time, the question of inverting organization titles in the cataloging of public documents came under fire and was investigated thoroughly. The decision was finally made that the alphabetic cataloging of public documents would be of no use at all if legal titles of government offices were used, since most of these titles begin with the word department, bureau, court, office, etc. Also, during the inquiry into entry policy, heads of offices interviewed acknowledged that even they did not know the legal designations of the organizations they were administering.

Thus, the confusion over legal name and the opinion of the majority of catalogers at the Public Documents Office led to the decision that the key or distinguishing word of the organization title would be used as a main entry; to secure this, the legal titles of these organizations would be inverted when necessary as had always been the practice.[3]

PRINCIPLES OF THE SYSTEM

General Principles

The basis of the classification is the grouping together of the publications of any government author—the various departments, bureaus and agencies being considered authors. The grouping follows the organizational structure of the United States government—that is, subordinate bureaus and divisions are grouped with the parent organization. Official entries are established by the item number cards (see Chapter 4) for depository items and these cards are amended by the "New Classification Numbers" section in the *Monthly Catalog*. The *Monthly Catalog* (or the Superintendent of Documents shelf list) provides the only official source of entries for non-depository publications.

A letter symbol is assigned for each executive department and agency, Congress, the judiciary, and major independent agencies. These symbols are based on the distinctive word or words of the agency's name—thus, "A" for Agriculture Department, "C" for Commerce Department, and "CS" for Civil Service Commission.

To set off the subordinate bureaus and agencies, numbers are added to the letters; number 1 is used for the parent organization and the secretary's or administrator's office. Beginning with the number "2" the numbers are applied in numerical order to the subordinate bureaus and offices, these having been arranged alphabetically when the system was established; new subordinate bureaus or offices are assigned the next highest number. A period follows the combinations of letters and numbers representing the bureau or office. For example:

Health, Education and Welfare Department (including the Secretary's Office)	HE 1.
Social Security Administration	HE 3.
Office of Education	HE 5.
Public Health Service	HE 20.

The next breakdown in this system is for the various series of publications issued by the agencies. Each series is assigned a number, which is followed by a colon. In the beginning the following numbers were assigned for the types of publications common to most government offices:

1: Annual reports
2: General publications (unnumbered publications of a miscellaneous nature)
3: Bulletins
4: Circulars

These numbers are still reserved for such publications as new agencies or bureaus set up. Later, new types common to most offices evolved and the following additional numbers were set aside in the classes of new agencies for particular types of series:

> 5: Laws (administered by the agency and published by it)
> 6: Regulations, rules, and instructions
> 7: Releases
> 8: Handbooks, manuals, guides

Any additional series issued by an office are given the next highest numbers in order of issuance—that is, as an office begins publication of a series, the next highest number not already assigned to a series is assigned to the new series of that particular office.

New series that are closely related to already existing series are now tied in to the existing series so that they file side by side on the shelf. Originally no provision was made for this except in the case of separates from publications in a series. Tie-in is provided by use of the shilling mark (slash) after the number assigned to the existing series, followed by a digit for each related series; these digits start with "2"; the "1" is not generally used in this connection since the existing series is the first. Separates are distinguished by use of a lower case letter (beginning with "a") rather than by numbers. A theoretical example of these "tie-in" classes is as follows:

> 4: Circulars
> 4/a: Separates from Circulars (numbered)
> 4/b: Separates from Circulars (unnumbered)
> 4/2: Administrative Circulars
> 4/3: Technical Circulars

The combination of an author symbol and series symbol is called the class stem of a particular series. For example:

> HE 1.1: Annual Report of the Secretary of Health, Education and Welfare
> HE 3.52: Social Security Information Series
> HE 5.25: Education Directory

The individual book number follows the colon. For numbered series the original edition of a publication gets simply the number of the book. For example, the second publication in HEW's Consumer Information Series (HE 1.34/2:) would have a book number of HE 1.34/2:2. For revisions or subsequent editions of the same publication, the shilling mark and additional figures beginning with "2" are added (e.g., HE 1.34/2:2/2, HE 1.34/2:2/4).

For annual publications, the last three digits of the year are used for the book number—e.g., the *Annual Report of the Secretary of Health, Education, and Welfare, 1973* would be HE 1.1:973. Publications that cover more than a year carry a book number designation such as LC 33.9:951-61 for *Antarctic Bibliography, 1951-1961* published by the Library of Congress.

Unnumbered publications (other than continuations) are given a book number based on the principal subject word of the title, using a 2-figure Cutter table. An example is *Radioactive Heating of Vehicles Entering the Earth's Atmosphere*, NAS 1.2:R11; "radioactive" is the key subject word, and the Cutter designation is R11. Another publication, *Measurements of Radiation from Flow Fields of Bodies*

Flying Speeds Up to 13.4 Kilometers Per Second, issued by the same agency, falls in the same series class (NAS 1.2:) and has the same Cutter number for the principal subject word; it is individualized by the addition of the shilling mark and the number 2—that is, NAS 1.2:R11/2. Subsequent different publications in the same subject group which take the same Cutter designation would be identified as R11/3, R11/4, etc.

The 3-figure Cutter table is used to assign book numbers to unnumbered separates or reprints from whole publications. This is done to provide finer distinctions in class between publications whose principal subject words begin with the same syllable. The 3-figure table is also sometimes used in regular unnumbered series for the same purpose.

Revisions of unnumbered publications are identified by addition of the shilling mark and the last three digits of the year of revision. For example, if the first publication mentioned above was revised in 1964, the complete classification number would be NAS 1.2:R11/964. Subsequent revisions in the same year would be identified as 964-2, 964-3, etc.

Periodicals and other continuations are identified by number, or volume and number as the case may be. Volume and number are separated by use of the shilling mark. Some examples are:

Current Export Bulletin, No. 732 (C 42.11/2:732)
Marketing Information Guide, volume 17, number 1 (C 41.11:17/1)

Unnumbered periodicals and continuations are identified by the year of issuance and order of issuance throughout the year. The last three digits of the year are used, and a number corresponding to the order of issuance within the year is added, the two being separated by the shilling mark. An example is:

Urban Renewal Directory, December 31, 1971 (HH 7.8/2:971/2)

Publications Requiring Special Treatment

While the foregoing principles and rules govern the classification of the publications and documents of most government authors, the publications of certain agencies require special treatment. Most important of these are the classes assigned to:

1. Boards, commissions, and committees established by act of Congress or under authority of act of Congress, not specifically designated in the executive branch of the government nor as completely independent agencies.

2. Congress and its working committees.

3. Multilateral international organizations in which the United States participates.

4. Publications of the President and the Executive Office of the President including committees and commissions established by executive order and reporting directly to the President.

Boards, commissions and committees established by act of Congress or under authority of act of Congress, not specifically designated in the executive branch of the government nor as completely independent agencies, are grouped under one of the agency symbols assigned to congressional publications—namely, Y 3. This place in the scheme is reserved for all such agencies. The classification numbers of the publications of these agencies are then literally pushed over to the right: instead of the series designation, the individual agency designation follows the period. This agency designation is the Cutter author number from the 2-figure table for the first main word of the agency name, followed by the colon. Thus, the agency designation for the Atomic Energy Commission is Y 3.At7: and Y3.Sc4: is the agency designation for the Selective Service System. The shilling mark and numbers are used to distinguish between author designations of agencies having the same or similar first principal word in their names, such as Y 3.F31/8: for Federal Deposit Insurance Corporation and Y 3.F31/13: for Federal Inter-Agency River Basin Committee.

Series designations for publications of these agencies then follow the colon instead of preceding it. These series designations are assigned in the regular way.

Individual book numbers are then added to the series designations with no separation if the individual book numbers begin with letters, and are separated by the shilling mark if they begin with numbers. Thus, the Annual Report of the Atomic Energy Commission for the year 1961 is Y 3.At7:1/961, while the unnumbered AEC Report on Status Centrifuge Technology is classed as Y 3.At7:2G21.

The working committees of Congress (such as Appropriations, Judiciary, etc.), are grouped under one of the agency symbols assigned to Congress—namely, Y 4. As in the case of the Y 3. classifications discussed above, an author designation based on the name of the committee follows the period and is followed by the colon. Thus, the House Committee on Judiciary is Y 4.J89/1: and the Senate Committee on Judiciary is Y 4.J89/2:, the shilling mark and numbers 1 and 2 being used to distinguish between the two committees. If other committees were to be appointed and have the word "judiciary" as the principal subject word of their name, J89/3:, J89/4:, etc., would be used as the author designations.

No regular numbered series designations are normally used after the colon for the publications of the congressional committees since they are for the most part simply unnumbered hearings or committee prints. These are assigned book numbers by use of the 2-figure Cutter tables based on the principal subject word of the title of each, as for unnumbered publications in the regular classification scheme.

Where series do occur within the publications of a committee they have been treated in various ways. For example, the *Congressional Directory* has been given a series designation of "1" following the colon—Y 4.P93/1:1. Individual book numbers are then marked off by use of the shilling mark following the series designation, such as Y 4.P93/1:1/ with the particular issue being designated by Congress and session, Y 4.P93/1:1/91-2. Another example is the periodical *Economic Indicators*, which is issued by the Joint Economic Committee. It has been assigned a place in the group of publications issued by the Committee by using a Cutter designation after the colon (instead of the regular numerical series designation), based on the subject word "economic." Thus, the class stem is Y 4.Ec7:Ec7. Numbers for individual issues are then designated by year and number corresponding to the month of issue. So the issue of January 1963 would be Y 4.Ec7:Ec7/963-1. Congressional bills, documents, and reports are numbered series that are not given a place in the scheme by use of lettered symbols but that are simply filed at the end of all other classifications by Congress, session, and individual number; abbreviations are used for the series titles. The order of filing and manner of designation is as follows:

Series	Individual Examples
Senate Bills	91-2:S.528
House Bills	91-2:H.R.15961
Senate Joint Resolutions	91-2:S.J.Res.172
House Joint Resolutions	91-2:H.J.Res.1098
Senate Concurrent Resolutions	91-2:S.Con.Res.70
House Concurrent Resolutions	91-2:H.Con.Res.578
Senate Resolutions	91-2:S.Res.304
House Resolutions	91-2:H.Res.108
Senate Reports	91-2:S.rp.885
House Reports	91-2:H.rp.983
Senate Documents	91-2:S.doc.82
House Documents	91-2:H.doc.342

Multilateral international organizations in which the United States participates often issue publications that are published simultaneously by the United States. The U.S. portions of these organizations may also publish separately—for example, the United States National Commission for Unesco. Since U.S. participation in the United Nations falls in the realm of foreign relations, such publications are classed under the State Department. The two main class designations assigned are as follows:

S 3.   Arbitrations and Mixed Commissions to Settle International Disputes
S 5.   International Congresses, Conferences, and Commissions

The individual organizations are then treated as subordinate bureaus or offices. A number is assigned to each as it begins to publish, but the number follows the period rather than preceding it as in regular class construction. Individual book numbers are assigned after the colon, using the 2-figure Cutter table and based on the principal subject word of the title.

Publications of the president and the Executive Office of the President (including committees and commissions established by executive order and reporting directly to the president) are treated in a different manner because of their different nature. The agency symbol assigned to the President of the United States is Pr followed by the number corresponding to the original number of succession to the presidency. Thus, Pr 37. for Richard M. Nixon, 37th President of the United States. Breakdowns under the agency symbol follow normal methods of classification expansion. In recent years, however, presidents have appointed many special committees and commissions to study particular problems and to report their findings directly to the chief executive. These organizations usually cease to exist after making their report. Since their publications are usually few in number, normal bureau treatment is not practical. Special treatment is therefore indicated to prevent the establishment of classes that will not be used, and also to keep together the publications of all such organizations appointed by one president.

Beginning with those organizations established by President Eisenhower, one series class (Pr — .8:) has been assigned for all such committees and commissions. A Cutter designation using the 2-figure table is then assigned to each based on the principal subject word of its name (such as Pr 34.8:H81 for the President's Advisory Committee on Government Housing Policies and Programs). Publications of the committee are distinguished by addition of the shilling mark and Cutter numbers based on the principal subject word of the titles, as in normal classification.

Beginning with the administration of President Kennedy, the continuing offices assigned to the president, which make up the Executive Office of the President, have been given permanent classes under the symbol PrEx. A change in administration no longer makes it necessary to change the classes for such offices as the National Security Council and the Council of Economic Advisors. These have been given breakdowns as subordinate offices of the Executive Office of the President—for example, the Consumer Affairs Office is PrEx 16. Series and book numbers are then assigned in the usual manner.

**ADVANTAGES AND DISADVANTAGES
OF THE SYSTEM**

The pros and cons of the SuDocs system have been discussed for years. The key advantages, which are mentioned repeatedly, are 1) classification numbers appear on the daily depository shipping lists, which allows for immediate handling and shelving by the library staff and use by library patrons; 2) classification numbers correlate with established indexes and bibliographies such as the *Monthly Catalog* and *Price Lists*; and 3) the *Monthly Catalog* may be used as the subject index to the collection, thereby saving libraries the cost of subject cataloging.

The following appear to be the primary disadvantages of the SuDocs system: 1) Frequent changes in classification numbers due to reorganization of the government make it difficult to keep series together. An example of this is the publication *Children Today*, issued by the U.S. Child Development Office with the number HE 21.9^2. The publishing history of this is as follows:

L5.35:	U.S. Children's Bureau The child, monthly news summary v.1-10; July 1935-June 1946
FS 3.207:	The child v.11-18; July 1946-Dec. 1953
FS 3.207/2:	Children v.1-9; 1954-1963
FS 14.109:	v.10-14, no.4; March 1963-Aug. 1967

FS 17.209:   v.14, no.5-v.16; Sept. 1967-1969

HE 21.9:   U.S. Child Development Office
                                              Children
                                              v.17-v.18, no.6; 1970-1971

HE 21.9/2:   Children Today
                                              v.1, no.1– ; 1972–

2) Classification of non-depository items is frequently delayed because of the long time lapse between their distribution and their entry in the *Monthly Catalog*. Some publications, such as committee prints, do not appear for from four months to a year or are never listed. 3) Classification of non-depository items sometimes has to be handled by the library; since such items are printed outside the Government Printing Office, they are never entered in the *Monthly Catalog*. 4) Entries for new depository series or changes in series designations are not always indicated on shipping lists, and sometimes there is a delay of several months before the *Monthly Catalog* establishes the final entry, so record keeping is a problem. 5) Some series have publications that fall into a subseries grouping, and these are not brought out clearly by the classification scheme. This is exemplified by the publications of the committees and commissions of the president. The official entry is:

U.S. President.
Committees and Commissions of the President.

This entry does not allow one to locate the publications of a specific committee by committee name, so processing and reference service become problems. 6) Locating classification numbers for publications that are interdepartmental in nature is often difficult and causes much delay in processing. The general rule is to assign the number of the agency that initiated the project, rather than of an agency that carried out the work. At the present time, this principle is violated often enough to cause hesitation in assuming an entry. For example, C 3.186: P23/no.38 is entitled *The Social and Economic Status of Negroes in the United States, 1970*. The title page shows it to be Bureau of Labor Statistics Report No. 394 *and* Census Bureau Current Population Reports, Series P-23, No. 38.
7) The scheme is good only for federal publications. Since most segregated collections are responsible for a number of kinds of government publications, multiplicity of classification schemes must be used within the department.

In summarizing the key issues of the Superintendent of Documents Classification System, it must be said that the economic advantages of having a ready-made index (the *Monthly Catalog*) and the immediate availability of classification numbers for depository items (which consist of over 70 percent of most federal documents collections) have caused increasing numbers of major depository libraries to move to the separate collection using the Superintendent of Documents Classification System. The problems inherent in the system are not insurmountable, especially in light of the problems inherent in other systems (which are discussed in Chapter 9). Many methods have been developed to overcome each of the disadvantages mentioned in this chapter, and these are presented in the various chapters of this manual. Once the decision has been made to utilize the system, the necessary modifications can be made using these guidelines and common sense, in conjunction with a knowledge of the library's situation.

FOOTNOTES

[1] U.S. Documents Office. *Monthly Catalogue of United States Public Documents, No. 210, June 1912.* (Washington, Government Printing Office, 1912) pp. 821-23.

[2] U.S. Public Documents Department. *An Explanation of the Superintendent of Documents Classification System.* Rev. Washington, Government Printing Office, 1970.

[3] U.S. Documents Office. *Monthly Catalogue of United States Public Documents, loc. cit.*

Chapter 3

BIBLIOGRAPHIC CONTROL OF
GOVERNMENT DOCUMENTS

Government and commercially published reference sources are available to help documents librarians fully utilize their collections. Because documents encompass such a wide array of subjects and because they are not as easily located as other books housed in the library's collection, documents indexes and bibliographies are necessary tools. Every documents librarian should be fully cognizant of what these sources are, when to use them, and what they contain. It is not the purpose of this chapter to provide a comprehensive bibliography of sources but simply to point out the major ones and their functions within the framework of bibliographic control and reference service.

RETROSPECTIVE GOVERNMENT SOURCES

The earliest attempt at bibliographic control of documents was made by Benjamin Perley Poore. His *Descriptive Catalogue of the Government Publications of the United States, September 5, 1774-March 4, 1881* (GPO, 1885. 1,392p.) constitutes a chronological listing of publications from the judicial, legislative, and, especially, congressional branches of the federal government. The quality of Poore's work leaves a lot to be desired, but despite many discrepancies, omissions, and a very poor index, Poore's *Descriptive Catalogue* remains the only source for locating the earlier publications.

John Griffith Ames's *Comprehensive Index to the Publications of the United States Government, 1881-1893* (GPO, 1905. 2v. 1,590p.) is a subject listing of government documents published from 1881 to 1893. Because the subject headings are essentially key words in titles, they are inconsistent, and cross references are not provided. But it is the only source for the period and does fill the gap between Poore and the *Document Catalog*.

A section of the Printing Act of 1895 (discussed in Chapter 1) called for a comprehensive index of all public documents to be published at the end of each session of Congress. In 1896, the first volume of *Catalog of the Public Documents of Congress and of All Departments of the Government* was issued. Better known as the *Document Catalog*, this guide was published biennially until 1945. The first issue covered documents published in 1893 and the final year covered was 1940. This is a dictionary catalog with entries for subjects, personal and departmental authors, and even some titles, with complete bibliographic citations provided. The time lag between the dates covered and the publication date, and increased printing costs, contributed to the decision to discontinue the *Document Catalog*.

Other important sources for historical research in government documents are described below:

Greely, General Adolphus Washington. *Public Documents of the First Fourteen Congresses, 1789-1817.* 1900. 56th Cong. 1st Sess. Doc. 428.

Contains, with index, 903 pages. Lists around 5,000 state papers. Arranged by Congress and Session, Chamber and series in chronological order. Contains brief annotations, with location of document.

Greely, General Adolphus Washington. *Public Documents of the First Fourteen Congresses, 1789-1817.* Supplement. American Historical Association, Annual report, v. 1, 1903, pp. 343-406.

Describes and locates 754 Congressional papers. Approximately half are titles not previously listed.

Index to the Reports and Documents of the 54th Congress, 1st Session to 72d Congress, 2nd Session, Dec. 2, 1895-March 4, 1933, with numerical lists and schedule of volumes. 1897-1933.

Subject index to the Serial set for the period. Often called *Document Index*.

Tables of and Annotated Index to the Congressional Series of United States Public Documents. 1902. 769p.

Covers the publications of the first 25 Congresses. The subject index is a valuable asset for the publications of the period.

U.S. Superintendent of Documents. *Checklist of United States Public Documents, 1789-1909.* 3rd ed. Washington, Government Printing Office, 1911. Vol. 1.

Arranged by SuDocs numbers, it gives histories of agencies and cross references to earlier and later classifications. It includes a list of publishing agencies.

U.S. Superintendent of Documents. *The Monthly Catalog of U.S. Government Publications, 1895-1924.* Washington, Carrollton Press, 1974. (in progress).

This valuable reprint of earlier catalogs contains SuDocs numbers which the original *Monthly Catalog* did not have.

CURRENT GOVERNMENT SOURCES

Current sources of information about and/or guides to the literature in the public domain are many and varied. A selective list of those published by the government follows.

Monthly Catalog of United States Government Publications. Washington, GPO, 1895– . Monthly. This guide is indispensable for anyone working with U.S. government publications. It lists publications of all departments or agencies alphabetically by key word in issuing agency name (e.g., Census Bureau, not Bureau of the Census). Entries are numbered consecutively through each year with an index each month and a cumulative index in the December issue. Entries note publications available from the Superintendent of Documents or other sources. Full titles, personal authors, and complete bibliographical information are given in each entry. The *Monthly Catalog* is prepared in accordance with the Printing Act of 1895, and is a record of every publication received by the Library of the Public Documents Division of the Government Printing Office during the previous month. This is an obvious limitation. Despite attempts to record non-GPO publications, individual agencies do not always comply by sending copies of their documents to GPO. Thus, many are never listed in the *Monthly Catalog.* The value and usefulness of the *Monthly Catalog* cannot be underestimated, as it serves the same purposes for government publications as does the *Cumulative Book Index* for general book publications. GPO has published decennial cumulative indexes to the *Monthly Catalog* for the periods 1941-1950 and 1951-1960. Additionally, Pierian Press has published a very useful set of cumulative personal author indexes for the periods 1941-1950, 1951-1960, 1961-1965, and 1966-1970 and Carrollton Press has initiated a cumulative subject index for the period from 1900 to 1971.

The *Numerical Lists and Schedule of Volumes of the Reports and Documents of Congress* has been published annually since 1934; it is the key to the Serial set.

An equally important access tool is *Government Reports Announcements* and its accompanying *Government Reports Index.* Formerly called *U.S. Government Research and Development Reports*, this guide is necessary for locating technical data generated by the U.S. government. Publications listed and abstracted in GRA are available from the National Technical Information Service, as are subscriptions to the semi-monthly GRA and GRI.

Complimentary works are NASA's *Scientific and Technical Aerospace Reports (STAR)* and *Nuclear Science Abstracts* which index and abstract government and non-government research in their respective fields. There are indexes for corporate author, personal author, contract number, and accession number.

For education information, *Research in Education (RIE)* is essential. It indexes and abstracts publications of research done by individuals and institutions under government grant. Includes indexes by personal author, corporate author, grant number, and subject.

Selected U.S. Government Publications is a free, annotated guide to popular items published by GPO. Until 1974 it was published twice a month, but plans now call for monthly publication.

Another free bibliographical service has been the *Price Lists*, a series of booklets each limited to a given subject and listing in-print GPO publications (usually without annotations). Again, the 1974 shake-up at GPO has made a change. The *Price Lists* are to be discontinued and another series (as yet unnamed) will be issued.

GENERAL BIBLIOGRAPHIC GUIDES

Andriot, John L. *Guide to U.S. Government Serials and Periodicals.*
McLean, Va., Documents Index, 1962– . Annual.
Format varies from year to year, but each issue contains
essentially the same information. Arranged by SuDocs number, it
gives complete bibliographical information. Also included are item
numbers where appropriate, and beginning and ending dates. Most
important is its listing of many subseries not easily found elsewhere.
Volume one of the 1971 edition is an authority file for U.S. government
agencies and should be retained permanently as it has not been revised with
the rest of the set.

Body, Alexander C. *Annotated Bibliography of Bibliographies on
Government Publications.* Kalamazoo, Mich., the author, 1967.
Supplements 1968 and 1970.
Lists, with lengthy annotations, bibliographies published by
the federal government from 1958 through 1969. Arranged by
SuDocs number.

Boyd, Anne M. *United States Government Publications.* 3rd ed.,
rev. by Rae E. Ripps. New York, H. W. Wilson, 1949. 627p.
A standard tool, this guide provides information on the
history, organization, and functions of governmental agencies as
they pertain to printing, publishing, and distribution of documents. Indexed by subjects and titles.

*CIS/Index: Congressional Information Service/Index to the Pub-
lications of the United States Congress.* Washington, Congressional
Information Service, 1969– . Monthly (with quarterly and annual
cumulations).
Each monthly issue of the *CIS/Index* abstracts and indexes
hearings, reports, committee prints, and other congressional papers
issued during the previous month. Part one, the summary section,
lists and abstracts House committee publications, joint committee
publications, and Senate committee publications. One especially
valuable feature in this part is that virtually every item of individual
testimony of hearings is separately abstracted. Entries in this part
are by the CIS accession number system, which is fully explained in
the preface. Part two, the index section, contains indexes to subjects,
names, and bill, report, and document numbers. Annual cumulations
contain some data not in monthly issues or quarterly cumulations–
namely, brief descriptions and legislative histories of all Public Laws
enacted during the past year and a guide to multi-volume hearings
issued by Congress. Subscription prices are based on the book and
periodical budgets of individual libraries.

Checklist of United States Public Documents, 1789-1970: Indexes.
Comp. by Daniel and Marilyn Lester. Washington, United States
Historical Documents Institute, 1972. 5v.

These indexes are part of the dual media collection referred to
as Checklist '70. The fourth edition of the *Checklist* has been needed
for a long time (previous edition: GPO, 1911), and here it finally is,
complete with indexes. Checklist '70 (on 118 microfilm cartridges)
lists 1.2 million government publications in shelf list arrangement. It
is available with indexes for $2,550.00. The indexes are: 1) by SuDocs
number with government authors and organizations; 2) an alphabetical list of 3,000 government authors (both current and inactive); 3)
by key word of cabinet level departments subdivided by individual
publishing agencies, which are also listed alphabetically; 4) a list by
title of 18,000 series; and 5) the master key word index to the pub-
lications-issuing agencies. Each index entry gives both SuDocs and
microfilm reel numbers. These indexes are useful even without the
microfilm and are available separately for $160.00. Especially
valuable is volume two, which brings together all SuDocs numbers
for any government author regardless of its time in history or present
status. No depository library can afford to be without the fourth
edition of the *Checklist* and its indexes. Libraries with medium-sized
collections will find the indexes alone valuable in servicing documents.

*Government Reference Books: A Biennial Guide to U.S. Govern-
ment Publications.* Comp. by Sally Wynkoop. Littleton, Colo.,
Libraries Unlimited, Inc., 1970– . Biennial.

A classified list of government publications that have special
value as reference works. Entries in this comprehensive bibliography
are annotated and accessible through the detailed author, title, and
subject index.

Jackson, Ellen. *Subject Guide to Major United States Government
Publications.* Chicago, American Library Association, 1968. 175p.

Essentially a revision of *Subject Guide to United States Government Publications*, by Hirshberg and Melinat (Chicago, A.L.A.,
1947). Includes only GPO-published materials, listed under broad
subjects. Use of this work is hampered by the lack of an index.

Kyriak, Theodore E. *JPRS Catalog Cards in Book Form.*
Annapolis, Md., Research Microfilms, 1957/61-1968. New York,
CCM Information Corporation, 1969– .

Introduction each year gives background information on the
JPRS series. Arrangement of the volumes varies during the years,
but generally entries give JPRS number, code number for geographic
area, reel number for the publisher's microfiche service, and pagina-
tion. Inclusion of the title and page-by-page indexing for serials and
monographs makes this the best tool for general search. An index
adds to the effectiveness.

Kyriak, Theodore E. *Subject Index to U.S. Joint Publications Research Service Translations.* Annapolis, Md., Research and Microfilm Publications, Inc., 1966-1967. New York, CCM Information Science, Inc., 1968– .

Each semi-annual issue gives background information on one JPRS system. The index is arranged by subject. Items are indicated by geographic code number, issue number, and page. Cross-reference indexes locate the translation in the RMP Bibliography-Index, RMP microfilm reel number, and microfiche number.

Leidy, W. Philip. *A Popular Guide to Government Publications.* 3rd ed. New York, Columbia University Press, 1968. 365p.

Lists items of interest to a general audience in a subject arrangement. A fourth edition is in preparation.

Mechanic, Sylvia. *Annotated List of Selected United States Government Publications Available to Depository Libraries.* New York, H. W. Wilson, 1971. 407p.

This bibliography of nearly 500 entries arranged by item number (i.e., the number given to each series or group of publications available to depository libraries) is useful primarily in new depository libraries. Indexed by series or titles.

Pohle, Linda C. *A Guide to Popular Government Publications: For Libraries and Home Reference.* Littleton, Colo., Libraries Unlimited, Inc., 1972. 213p.

Contains over 2,000 annotated references to government publications that have wide appeal. The emphasis is on topics of current interest; most items included were published between 1968 and 1972. Includes an analytical subject index.

Schmeckebier, Laurence F., and Roy B. Eastin. *Government Publications and Their Use.* 2d rev. ed. Washington, Brookings Institution, 1969. 502p.

"The purpose of this volume is to describe the basic guides to government publications, to indicate the uses and limitations of available indexes, catalogs and bibliographies, to explain the system of numbering and methods used of titling, to call attention to certain outstanding compilations or series of publications, and to indicate how the publications may be obtained. It is thus a guide to the acquisition and use of government publications and not—even though it cites many publications by title—a catalog, a bibliography, or a checklist" (Foreword). Schmeckebier, a standard source since the first edition in 1936, is indispensable for those seeking to understand the form and style of U.S. government publishing activities.

Wisdom, Donald F., and William P. Kilroy. *Popular Names of U.S. Government Reports: A Catalog.* 2d ed. Washington, GPO, 1970.

This bibliography of reports of all branches of government is arranged by popular names and contains reproductions of Library of Congress printed cards, which show the correct form of entry. Indexed by subjects. A new edition in preparation will also give SuDocs number and *Monthly Catalog* entry citation.

Wood, Jennings, ed. *United States Government Publications: A Partial List of Non-GPO Imprints.* Chicago, American Library Association, 1964. 86p.

Lists nearly 1,700 publications issued by federal agencies and not distributed through the Government Printing Office. More recent information is contained in the Library of Congress' *Non-GPO Imprints Received in the Library of Congress*, which has been published annually since 1970 by the Library of Congress.

Wynkoop, Sally. *Subject Guide to Government Reference Books.* Littleton, Colo., Libraries Unlimited, Inc., 1972. 276p.

An annotated list of the most important reference books published by GPO and the various government agencies. Entries are arranged under broad subjects and are further classified by specific subjects. Indexed by personal author, title, and subject.

TOPICAL BIBLIOGRAPHIC GUIDES

The majority of the works which fall under the heading "topical bibliographic guides" are publications catalogs of the various U.S. government agencies and departments. These lists are very useful and should be at hand for anyone servicing government documents. Many of the non-GPO publications can be located through these lists and not through any other source. Often departments will issue catalogs, as will their subordinate agencies. For example, *United States Department of Commerce Publications* is published annually and the Census Bureau publishes its own quarterly catalog.

Some specialized trade publications on government documents have been issued in recent years. For example, Pestana's *Bibliography of Congressional Geology* (New York, Hafner, 1972) and Vinge's *U.S. Government Publications for Research and Teaching in Geography and Related Social and Natural Sciences* (Totowa, N.J., Littlefield, Adams, 1967).

Most recent, and, perhaps most ambitious, is *American Statistics Index: A Comprehensive Guide and Index to the Statistical Publications of the U.S. Government* (Washington, Congressional Information Service, 1973– . Annual with monthly supplements). The first annual issue indexes statistics pertaining to the American people—i.e., demographic data, vital and health statistics, etc. Expanded coverage (including the economic statistics of commerce, finance, government transactions, and natural resources) is planned for 1974. The purposes of ASI were succinctly stated in the pilot issue: "Identify the statistical data published by the Government; catalog the publications in which these data appear, providing full bibliographic information about each publication; describe the contents of these publications fully; announce new publications as they appear; index this information in full subject detail." This is actually more than just an index. Volume one of the two-volume 1973 edition lists publications with accession numbers, very complete bibliographic data, abstracts describing the publications, references to related works, technical notes, references to illustrative data, and titles and pages of individual statistical tables. Volume two contains indexes to subjects and personal and corporate names, to categories, and to titles and report numbers.

Documents librarians are in a unique position—they must be constantly aware of the activities of trade publishers as well as the publishing activities of the federal government. Furthermore, in order to be fully aware of the government's publishing activities, it is necessary to know the structure of the government itself. Staying abreast of the reorganization, restructuring, and shifting importance of government agencies, while maintaining an understanding of their histories, is not easy but it is worthwhile to the conscientious documents librarian. A knowledge of the tools discussed here and of other relevant sources will make the job somewhat easier.

Chapter 4

TYPES AND FORMS OF RECORDS

ESSENTIAL RECORDS

The number of records that a documents department maintains usually reflects the amount of bibliographic control considered necessary to allow patrons to make the best use of the collection without undue expense. With this in mind, then, three types of records have been found necessary for maintaining adequate bibliographic control of government publications shelved by the Superintendent of Documents Classification System. These are 1) an order file, 2) a shelf list, and 3) an item number file.

Order File

The necessity for maintaining an order file and the uses for such a file will be discussed in Chapter V, Acquisitions. The form to use for order cards will depend largely on the type of ordering system that the library as a whole maintains; however, this file, or a copy of this file, should appear in the documents area so that the librarian can quickly see what has been ordered and so that the mail can be checked to determine receipt.

Shelf List

The shelf list or holdings file is the absolute authority in the library for determining what materials are in the documents collection. This file will make it easy to determine whether an item has ever been available in the collection, and it is the only record of what has been received. This file should be arranged according to the Superintendent of Documents number; any deviation between the shelves and the shelf list should be noted on these cards. All item numbers and cross references should be noted on these cards in order to facilitate searching and reference service for each series. The shelf list cards are to be arranged in order by classification number. Types of cards used will depend on the frequency and form of the publication. If the first piece received as a depository item is not the first one in the series, then the card should indicate the first one received. This defines the point at which the library is responsible for the holdings.

Cuttered publications: If a publication is cuttered, then a plain white 3" x 5" index card will be used for the shelf list. On this card will appear the Superintendent of Documents Classification Number, U.S., name of the issuing agency (in the case of depository items, this is name that appears in all capital letters on the item number card), the title of the series, the title of the cuttered publication, and date of publication. If a number of cuttered publications are issued by the same agency under the same series title, then the cuttered publications will be arranged on one or more cards in alpha-numerical order.

Figure 4.1

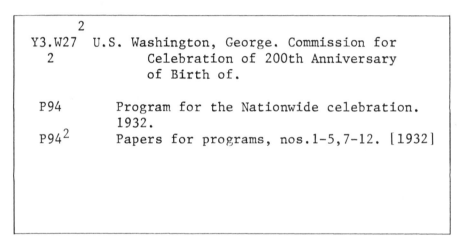

Figure 4.1 is an example of cuttered publications numbered consecutively, so that they can be entered on the same card. However, if they are not consecutively numbered, new cards must be made for each number—i.e., H34/12 *could not* appear on the card in Figure 4.1, nor could Ad9 nor In8. Using separate cards for each cutter number is a safe procedure.

An alternate method is to use a separate card for each piece received, with limited descriptive cataloging information. This would obviously take a great deal more time than the suggestions elaborated here and below, and an unlimited amount of space would have to be allowed for expansion of the shelf list.

Numbered and dated publications: If a publication appears annually, semi-annually, quarterly, monthly, semi-monthly, daily, weekly, etc., or in some continuing numbered sequence, then one of the shelf list cards shown below will be used, containing the Superintendent of Documents Classification Number, U.S., name of the issuing agency, and title.

Publications issued on an annual or semi-annual basis should be entered with check marks beside the year. Figure 4.2 shows holdings of the Library of Congress *Annual Report*; Figure 4.3 shows the library's holdings of NASA's *Semi-Annual Report* and also indicates that the series is numbered consecutively.

Figure 4.2

LC1.1 U.S. Library of Congress. Annual report.							
1951	1961	1971	1981	1991	2001	2011	2021
1952	1962	1972	1982	1992	2002	2012	2022
1953	1963	1973	1983	1993	2003	2013	2023
1954	1964	1974	1984	1994	2004	2014	2024
1955	1965	1975	1985	1995	2005	2015	2025
1956	1966	1976	1986	1996	2006	2016	2026
1957	1967	1977	1987	1997	2007	2017	2027
1958	1968	1978	1988	1998	2008	2018	2028
1959	1969	1979	1989	1999	2009	2019	2029
1960	1970	1980	1990	2000	2010	2020	2030

Figure 4.3

NAS1.1 U.S. National Aeronautics and Space Administration. Semi-annual report.							
1951	1961 5/6	1971	1981	1991	2001	2011	2021
1952	1962 7/8	1972	1982	1992	2002	2012	2022
1953	1963 9/10	1973	1983	1993	2003	2013	2023
1954	1964 11/12	1974	1984	1994	2004	2014	2024
1955	1965 13/14	1975	1985	1995	2005	2015	2025
1956	1966 15/16	1976	1986	1996	2006	2016	2026
1957	1967 17/18	1977	1987	1997	2007	2017	2027
1958	1968 19/20	1978	1988	1998	2008	2018	2028
1959 no. 1/2	1969 21/22	1979	1989	1999	2009	2019	2029
1960 3/4	1970	1980	1990	2000	2010	2020	2030

Index 1958-69

Entries on cards used for quarterly, or more frequently issued publications, should match what is used on the publication itself. In Figure 4.4 the month is checked because it is used on the periodical.

Figure 4.4

Y4.Ec7 Ec7	U.S. Congress. Economic Joint Committee Economic indicators.													
Yr.	Vol.	Ja.	F	Mr.	Ap.	My.	Je.	Jl.	Ag.	S	O	N	D	T. P. and I.
1970		✓	✓	✓	✓	✓	✓	✓	✓	✓	✓	✓	✓	
1971		✓	✓	✓	✓	✓	✓	✓	✓	✓	✓	✓	✓	
1972		✓	✓	✓	✓	✓	✓	✓	✓	✓	✓	✓	✓	
1973		✓	✓											

Periodicals shown in Figures 4.5 and 4.6 are identified by volume and number; therefore, these are indicated on the shelf list cards.

Figure 4.5

D101.47	U.S. Army Department. Army aviation digest.													
Yr.	Vol.	Ja.	F	Mr.	Ap.	My.	Je.	Jl.	Ag.	S	O	N	D	T. P. and I.
1971	17	1	2	3	4	5	6	7	8	9	10	11	12	
1972	18	1	2	3	4	5	6	7	8	9	10	11	12	
1973	19	1	2	3										

Figure 4.6

Yr.	Vol.	Ja.	F	Mr.	Ap.	My.	Je.	Jl.	Ag.	S	O	N	D	T. P. and √
1970	27	1			2			3			4			✓
1971	28	1			2			3			4			✓
1972	29	1			2			3			4			✓
1973	30	1			2			3			4			✓

LC1.17   U.S. Library of Congress.
The quarterly journal of the Library of Congress.

Title was formerly Quarterly journal of acquisitions

Figure 4.7 illustrates a holdings card used for daily or weekly periodicals.

Figure 4.7

T1.5   U.S. Treasury Department.
1973   Daily statement of the U.S. Treasury.

Library Form No. 25 ⚹ *Claimed 3.26.73*

Numbered publications can be entered by check marks beside the number as shown in Figure 4.8. This example also shows which was the first received as a depository item.

Figure 4.8

```
NAS1.19  U.S. National Aeronautics and Space
                Administration.
          NASA EP (series)

no. 7 is 1963
```

✓1	✓11	✓21	✓31	✓41	51	61	✓71	✓81	✓91
✓2	✓12	✓22	✓32	✓42	52	62	✓72	✓82	✓92
✓3	13	23	✓33	✓43	53	63	✓73	✓83	✓93
4	✓14	24	✓84	✓44	54	✓64	74	✓84	✓94
✓5	15	✓25	✓85	✓45	55	65	✓75	✓85	95
✓6	✓16	26	✓36	✓46	56	✓66	✓76	86	✓96
*✓7	✓17	✓27	37	✓47	57	67	✓77	✓87	✓97
8	18	✓28	✓38	✓48	58	✓68	✓78	✓88	98
9	19	29	39	49	59	69	✓79	✓89	99
✓10	20	✓30	✓40	✓50	30	✓70	80	✓90	00

```
* No. 7 is 1st dep.
```

Regardless of the type of card used, the item number of all depository series must appear on the back of the card. This allows a quick cross reference and it is an essential aid in completing all records when verification of entry and of classification number is made. Because this information is permanent, it should be typed.

Item Number File

In 1950, a major revision of the *Classified List of U.S. Government Publications* was prepared in a 3" x 5" card format. This card was called the item number card, and the files associated with these cards are the item number files. Each item number card (see Figure 4.9) contains the verified main entry and title for every depository series as they have been established by the catalogers of the Library of the Public Documents Division. The cards are intended as a semi-permanent list that can be amended to provide for new depository series as they are created. For most effective use, these cards should be arranged in numerical order in their file. If the library is only a selective depository, this file will have two parts: 1) items received and 2) items not received. The cards for the series not selected should be kept by selective depositories, so that series not originally deemed appropriate for inclusion in the collection may be added as the need arises. The item number file is one that must be absolutely accurate. To maintain a complete record of selections, the individual library must generate its own item card to reflect such changes and additions. The date of selection, shipping list number, and *Monthly Catalog* citation should be noted on the item number cards.

Figure 4.9

Item No. 610-A[1]

NATIONAL MARINE FISHERIES SERVICE[2]

Shellfish Situation and Outlook[4]   C55.309/4[3]

SL 5778; 12.7.70[5]

Feb. 1971 MC[6]

[1] Item Number
[2] Government Author
[3] SuDocs Number
[4] Series Title
[5] Shipping List Number and Date
[6] First Entered in *Monthly Catalog*

The complete depository returns one item number card for each item number; the selective depository returns one card for each series it wishes to receive and files the cards of series which is does not want in the "item numbers not received" file. The cards for series received are then filed in the "items received" file by item number.

Many separate series may be included under one item number. Although it is not often explained, a library can elect to receive only one series from an item number. However, it is necessary to take all of whatever series is chosen. Figure 4.9 and 4.10 illustrate one item number which is comprised of several series.

Note that a separate item number card exists for each series within that item number. Libraries electing to receive only one or two series from that number will file those cards in the "items received" file. The other cards will be filed in the "items not received" file.

OPTIONAL RECORDS

Other records which many libraries have found useful are the 1) main entry or author file, 2) series title file, 3) subscriptions file, 4) bound volume status file, and 5) main entry "items not received" file arranged by main entry.

Figure 4.10

```
Item No. 610-A



        NATIONAL MARINE FISHERIES SERVICE
Frozen Fish Report                            C55.309

          SL 5770; 12.1.70

Feb. 1971 MC
```

```
Item No. 610-A



        NATIONAL MARINE FISHERIES SERVICE
Current Fishery Statistics (CFS series)   C55.309/2

          SL 5770; 12.1.70

Jan. 1971 MC
```

```
Item No. 610-A



        NATIONAL MARINE FISHERIES SERVICE
Food Fish Situation and Outlook            C55.309/5

            SL 5781; 12.9.70

Feb. 1971 MC
```

Main Entry or Author File

The main entry file, or author file, can be a useful tool for establishing classification numbers for new materials or for reference service to patrons who know the author of the series for which they are looking. This file is a record of all series received by the library, and the entries are those established by the item number cards or the "New Classification Numbers" section of the *Monthly Catalog*. Cross references on these cards help the librarian to search efficiently for a publication in the stacks or shelf list. These cards should be arranged in alphabetical order so as to provide a complementary file to the shelf list.

Figure 4.11 is an example of a main entry or author file card. Note that the SuDocs number, main entry, title (and cross references as needed), are typed on the card.

Figure 4.11

```
D214.10   U.S. Marine Corps.
          Reserve Marine.
```

Series Title File

The series title file is a record of all series with distinctive titles maintained by the library. The series title is taken from the item number cards or the *Monthly Catalog*. It is useful in searching for document numbers and in helping patrons find publications for which they already know the series without having to go through the *Monthly Catalog*. Figure 4.12 shows that on these cards the documents number, series title, main entry are typed. All cross references should also appear on the title file cards. This file should be arranged in alphabetical order.

Chapter 7, "Specialized Processes," and Chapter 8, "Optional Processes," give detailed instructions for elaboration of these two cards (Figures 4.11 and 4.12) when the series changes in any way. Agency, title, and classification changes can be shown on a single card to give the complete history of the publication.

Figure 4.12

```
D214.10        Reserve Marine.
       U.S. Marine Corps.
```

Subscriptions File

A third optional file would be the subscriptions file. Arranged by title, this file can give immediate information for every serial ordered. Depository titles can be listed here with that notation. Titles of all other serials should appear. Provision should be made (as shown in Figure 4.13) to indicate on the front of the card the call number, title, issuing agency, department receiving, date ordered, price, order or account number, dates covered by subscription; on the back of the card are the addresses of the receiver and of the sender.

Figure 4.13—Front of Card

Call No. PrEx 10.2: P94 changed to PrEx 2.20
Title   Catalog of federal domestic assistance

Issuing Agency   U.S. Economic Opportunity Office

Dept.   Arch 361.6: Un32

Ordered   5.19.71   4.11.72

Begins	1971 ed	1972 ed			
Expires	1 yr	1 yr			
Price	7.25	2.50 7.00			
Subs. no.	4112				
Acct no.	51346	51346 also binder			

Figure 4.13—Back of Card

```
University Address
   COFA  40506 GOVEROOOGC  51346D
   Government Publications Dept.
   Library Univ of Kentucky
   Lexington  Ky  40506

Publishers Address

GPO
```

Bound Volume Status File

The least essential file is the one that shows the status of binding of series. This is known as the bound volume status file. As individual pieces are received, the shelf list records their acquisition. But many of the serials are later collected and bound. A library may bind several items in a numbered series into one book, or it may divide a serial into more than one part and bind separately. More than one volume may be put in a single binding. The list that tells the physical volumes on the shelf, then, is valuable to the shelver, to the page, and to the circulation section.

Figure 4.14 is one example. It shows that some numbers in the series are bound separately (1797, 1799), some bound together (1801-1804), and that one book is bound in two sections (1809, A-J; 1809, K-U).

Figure 4.15 shows that there are several unbound volumes in the series. Spaces are left so that if these are later bound, the file can be altered to reflect this change.

Not-Received File

The not-received file, arranged by main entry, is not as common as the files described above, but it should be mentioned. Some large libraries have found that

Figure 4.14

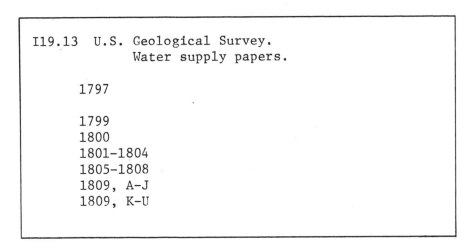

```
I19.13   U.S. Geological Survey.
              Water supply papers.

     1797

     1799
     1800
     1801-1804
     1805-1808
     1809, A-J
     1809, K-U
```

Figure 4.15

```
I19.16   U.S. Geological Survey.
              Professional papers.

     600                    641
     601-604
                            643

     610-612
     613                    650
     614
```

keeping a record of all new classification numbers assigned by the Superintendent of Documents saves much time in searching for new entries.

Before 1967, Mary E. Poole's *Documents Office Classification to 1966*, Edition 3, provided an authority for most main entries and series titles used by the Superintendent of Documents. Since 1966, the most easily accessible authority available is the "New Classification Numbers" section of the *Monthly Catalog*, which must be searched by the year until the documents number is found. The latest attempt to provide coverage is a series prepared by the United States Historical Documents Institute. The *Checklist of United States Public Documents 1789-1970*, a Dual Media Edition of the U.S. Superintendent of Documents' Public Documents Library Shelf List with five accompanying indexes, provides a multi-faceted approach to the identification and the classification of documents. A semi-annual update from October 1970 keeps this a current awareness tool. Daniel and Marilyn Lester are compiling *United States Government Serial Publications, 1789-1972*. They have, in computer printout, *A Preliminary Edition*, which is an attempt to locate and define all serials of all agencies of the government, and not just those cataloged by the Superintendent of Documents.

The main entry not received file allows one to search for the entry of any publication that has not previously appeared in the library. If this file is kept, it should be in the form of main entry cards arranged in alphabetical order. These cards would usually be typed from the "New Classification Numbers" section of the *Monthly Catalog* as a current working tool. Poole's and the U.S. Historical Documents Institute's listings would then be the source for older series.

Chapter 5

ACQUISITIONS

SOURCES OF FREE DOCUMENTS

The methods used to obtain government documents (other than those received as depository items) are almost as varied as the types of publications. It has been said that only the naive and uninitiated pay for public documents. While this may be an exaggeration, it is nevertheless true that means exist for obtaining free publications if one has the time, knowledge, and patience to pursue them. The sources of free publications discussed below should be tried or at least considered before an item is ordered from SuDocs or a commercial outlet.

Departmental Depository Systems

A number of departments and agencies have established their own depository systems. There is no one list of such establishments, nor even a list of the agencies that participate in a program of this kind. In addition, the agencies are under no legal obligations to continue with this method of distribution, so the list changes with time. Some do not call their programs "depository," but the idea is essentially the same.

Each agency has its own standards for inclusion in this automatic distribution system and each sets forth its own regulations. Some require an annual request for participating, with or without the demand that the institution have a government contract in its sphere of expertise. Others are established on a permanent basis.

There is diversity also in the types of publications available on a depository basis. The agency may distribute only the material that is available from GPO, or only major series, or it may include processed materials ephemeral in character, or microformat—or any combination of these categories.

Among those that either now or in the immediate past have presented such a program are the Bureau of the Census, the Department of Agriculture, the Geological Survey, the Atomic Energy Commission, the National Aeronautics and Space Administration, the Housing and Urban Development Department, the Public Health Service, the Manpower Administration of the Labor Department, the Patent

Office, and the Coast and Geodetic Survey. As specific examples, the Census Bureau and Geological Survey maintain depository lists. These vary in intent, scope, and availability. The Bureau of the Census explains its depository system as a means of supplementing the GPO system. The purpose is insuring that a collection of Census Bureau reports is available for reference and research at points relatively convenient to everyone. The Bureau of the Census furnishes copies of its reports to additional libraries, designated as Census Depository Libraries. These libraries were chosen on the basis of population (in the case of a city library), or enrollment (in the case of a college or university library), as well as on the basis of distance from the nearest Government Depository Library. The two depository systems make it possible for a collection of Census reports to be available in every important research center. The Geological Survey has explained that libraries meeting the criteria will be eligible for its map depository system. This system is selective not only for types of libraries but also for types of materials sent to those libraries.

Agency Mailing Lists

Most agencies maintain mailing lists for free distribution of materials. The materials available vary with the agency. Some send selected materials in a specified number of areas of interest, some send any material requested; a library may request all materials published by that agency. Almost all agencies require that the library return a form asking for continuance of its status, as the Joint Committee on Printing demands periodic accounting of the publishing and distributing programs of the agencies.

Members of Congress

Members of Congress may also be able to acquire an otherwise hard-to-get item. A letter to the representative of the library's Congressional district or to a Senator can tap a quick and almost sure supply. Members are allotted specified numbers of titles in current circulation. Most congressmen are only too willing to accommodate their constituency.

Congressional Committees

Congressional committees frequently maintain mailing lists to allow for automatic distribution of materials emanating from their activities. Congressional hearings are almost certainly distributed to those on the list. Committee prints are more often than not a part of the program. Since these are among the items that are hardest to get, inclusion on the list is important. Documents and reports are less often available in this way.

Library of Congress

The Library of Congress maintains an extensive Exchange and Gifts Program. Old and new publications of practically any component of government, with the exception of highly technical research literature, are available from this source. This service is to be used primarily for filling gaps in the collection, or for replacing lost or torn books, or for acquiring extra copies of a title. It is not intended as a source of current information.

A little-known aspect of this program is the availability of the Exchange and Gifts stacks to librarians. Any qualified librarian may request and receive a letter from a congressman to the Exchange and Gifts Section; this letter allows the librarian to search freely through the open stacks and select as much free material as desired. Franking labels from the congressman will then allow the Library of Congress staff to mail these materials free of charge to the home library.

To gain access to the closed stacks of this section, a library must have an account with the Library of Congress and must authorize a staff member to charge against that account. Then the designated staff member may search the closed stacks (these are better materials that have not already been picked through), select materials desired, and bid on the books. If the bid is accepted, the amount of the bid will be subtracted from the deposit account and the books will be mailed free, with Congressional franking labels, to the home library.

Exchange

One fruitful source of information on old and hard-to-get items is the exchange list. Regional depositories are circulating such lists more and more as the depositories in their respective states decide to relinquish older and/or less used materials. Also, government publications may be listed along with other types of materials offered for gifts or exchange.

If the lists are arranged in any kind of order, it is not too difficult to check against a shelf list to select needed titles. If items are merely listed in a haphazard fashion, however, it may be more trouble than it would be worth.

Generally, such titles are offered on a first-come, first-served basis. The cost of the postage is requested, and there is sometimes a request for a return list of material available from the receiving library.

SOURCES FOR PURCHASING DOCUMENTS

Once these sources of free publications have been exhausted, the remaining alternative is to purchase the publication. Orders may be placed through government sources or commercial services. The government sources are described below.

Documents Expediting Project

The Documents Expediting Project of the Library of Congress was initiated in 1946 by a group of librarians representing the American Library Association, the

American Association of Law Librarians, the Special Libraries Association and the Association of Research Libraries. The project was concerned with making non-depository materials more readily available to libraries and with making sure that one copy of each publication be sent to the Superintendent of Documents for cataloging and listing in the *Monthly Catalog*.

Libraries pay a subscription fee of from $175 to $525 and are entitled to services in proportion to the fee. The number of participating libraries has increased as the effectiveness of the program has grown.

The Project is the best source for printed copies of Congressional committee prints. It also distributes many out-of-print items, particularly from Congress. Requests for a particular title may be filled even after a considerable period of time if there is no immediately available copy.

The cost of this service seems well justified for a library attempting a sizeable collection. Priority for receipt of publications in short supply is based on a scale according to subscription fee paid and length of participation in the Project. For example, a library that pays an annual fee of $400 would gain in two ways by increasing its subscription to the $525 maximum. First, the library moves ahead of several other libraries on the priority list. Second, the position on the priority list cannot be lowered when other libraries join DocEx at higher rates. At the $400 rate, there is always the possibility that others would join DocEx at a higher subscription rate thereby lowering the library's position on the priority list.

Government Printing Office

The Government Printing Office was established to centralize the printing of documents, and the Superintendent of Documents was authorized to sell to the public such material as had been defined as being of general interest or educational value.

To effectuate this program, the GPO presents a number of current awareness tools. The *Monthly Catalog* is the major instrument for announcing those publications cataloged by the Library of the Superintendent of Documents. This gives complete bibliographic and acquisitions information. *Business Service Checklist*, *Selected Government Publications*, *Price Lists*, and flyers concerning single titles are other current awareness instruments.

National Technical Information Service (NTIS)

Research literature is announced in specialized indexes and abstracts. Since such reports are priced to assure that the publishing and sales organizations will be self-sustaining, prices of such reports will fluctuate.

NTIS is the chief arm of the government sales service of this material. While it is true that some agencies maintain their own sales services for very specialized types of material, it is still this central office that handles micro- and paper-copy purchase orders. Some programs are handled under contract, but indexes and abstracts will generally indicate such a source.

Commercial Services

Because there are so many ways for buying documents and several methods of paying, many libraries have resorted to using a commercial service to carry out their acquisitions program.

The services in general assert that it costs no more, or very little more, to use their good offices. The government allows discounts on publications bought in quantity. Thus, they claim, their cost is the difference between the discount they are allowed and the regular list price the single library would pay. This may, however, change drastically with new GPO sales policy changes.

If the only difficulty in purchasing documents were the multiplicity of form and source, most libraries would do their own acquisitions. It is the peculiarities of so very many agencies and titles that cause them to use a dealer.

One specific example will suffice. The *Survey of Current Business* is a monthly, available on subscription from GPO. Its weekly supplement, *Business Statistics*, is a part of that subscription. Its biennial supplement, *Business Statistics*, is not included, however, and must be ordered separately. Since GPO does not handle standing orders, the librarian must make a special effort to notice the publication announcement each two years. But this is not all. Numerous subject supplements to the *Survey* are published as monographs and are not covered by the subscription, so their relationship to the major title is not always clear. These subject supplements have been supplied by NTIS recently, so they are not listed in the *Monthly Catalog* with a Superintendent of Documents number.

Statistical Abstracts follows almost the same publication schedule. This annual must be ordered each year, and its supplements are sold completely apart from it.

Perhaps just as confusing are the serials that are on subscription but that have separately sold indexes. Thus, the peculiarities in serials and the great number of titles have helped further the growth of the sales services.

Some commercial services, such as Bernan Associates and C. & W. Associates, deal exclusively with government documents. But other dealers that might normally be used by the library, such as Baker and Taylor or Richard Abel, can also be used to obtain documents.

Microform and Reprint Companies

A casual glance at the *Monthly Catalog* over a few years will show that the number of titles is increasing by the year. And a comparison of the number of pages of almost any serial rather clearly indicates that periodicals are growing larger by the issue.

Restrictions on the number of copies printed of a given title stem from the economics of the sponsoring agency, from regulations of the Joint Committee on Printing, or from the policy of the GPO to print enough copies for only a given time period (one to five years).

The number of elementary and secondary schools, of colleges and universities and other educational institutions, and of public libraries increases steadily. These institutions have discovered the wealth of government material on an almost unlimited range of subjects on many levels of difficulty and complexity. They have also found that such sometimes definitive works are much cheaper than trade publications. These forces have combined to expand the depository system beyond its original concept and also to strain the physical and economical capabilities of established government presses.

The pressure of these elements has resulted in the proliferation of companies offering government material in microcopy and in reprint editions. There is little or no cooperation among such enterprises, and some of the major series and monographs are available in several forms of microform or reprint editions.

These commercially sponsored programs may be used to form a documents collection that is almost complete in major series from the beginning of the country's publications. The *American State Papers*, the Serial Set, the *Congressional Record* and its predecessors, the *Supreme Court Reports*, the hearings and committee prints of Congressional committees are only an indication of the range involved.

The Joint Committee on Printing has approved of the substitutions of microcopy for the original, if the microcopy is readily accessible and effectively served by available indexing tools. With this provision, many depositories are easing their space problems by substituting microcopies for the depository copy.

Out-of-Print Dealers

There will always be some people who believe that a book is the only medium useful in conveying information. Pragmatic scientists as well as dreaming philosophers will hold to this rule. As long as there are such readers, there will be a need for dealers who handle out-of-print material or material that is unusually hard to find.

Many o.p. dealers may have some documents hidden away among their wares. These appear, frequently with little or no descriptive notations, in the lists of their offerings. A few dealers will separate their documents from other types of material, but still without completely effective identifications.

Some dealers of out-of-print government documents are:

Q. M. Dabney
Box 32061
Temple Hills, Md. 20031

William Hein
Hein Bldg.
1285 Main St.
Buffalo, N.Y. 14009

Henry Tripp
Scientific Books and Periodicals
92-06 Jamaica Ave.
Woodhaven, N.Y. 11421

Samuel Ward
Government Publications
LaPlata, Md. 20646

This is not an attempt to define all of the methods or to delineate all of the sources for obtaining government documents. A study of publishers' catalogs and reviewing media will serve as further guides in identifying documents and in discovering the best kind of acquisitions program for a particular library.

BASIC ACQUISITIONS PROCEDURES

Details of the acquisitions process may change from library to library, but certain general procedures must be followed. When money is involved, it is imperative that accurate records be kept. Information about not only the amount spent but also the amount encumbered should be immediately available.

No matter what form is used, or what department places the order, pays the bills, or keeps the records, certain information is essential, such as author, title, place, publisher, date, price, vendor, date ordered, fund used, person and/or department requesting. In addition, LC card number, series notes, volume and number, pages, and editions should be listed as pertinent. This should be immediately visible on the front of the request form.

Other information must be added, but this can properly go on the back of the slip. Search information for verification of title prevents unnecessary duplication of work and also unnecessary duplication in the collection. Notes to the order clerk or others who will handle the publication expedite the handling of the order.

Government publications are acquired from a number of sources. Many distributors have their own regulations and procedures, which must be followed exactly. Other vendors will accept orders according to a library's own way. Thus, a multitude of methods are used for acquiring documents, and here again detailed instructions for each vendor should be at hand for consultation.

While the exact routines may vary with libraries, and the forms used for ordering may change, the principles will remain the same. Provisions for payment to be made and records of money spent will still be required; the same general bibliographic information will identify the piece to be acquired.

Receiving Requests

The front of the form shown in Figure 5.1a contains complete bibliographical data plus any special instructions. The reverse side (Figure 5.1b) indicates where the publication has been verified. It may have been in one of the standard sources, where correct entry is assumed or in some bibliography or listing not usually used for official entry. Knowledge of the source of the citation can help the librarian if insufficient information is listed by the requester.

If the request is for a departmental library and not the government documents department, it is first necessary to verify the main entry and to locate the Library of Congress card number so that the information will be available when the book is received and the cataloging procedure begins.

To establish LC entry, one must check the book (for either LC card number or sample LC entry), then check proof sheets, *National Union Catalog*, *Library of Congress Catalog*, and other standard sources. The source where the item was verified should be noted on the back of the request form.

A multiple copy order form (Figure 5.2) must be filled out for each item being requested for departmental libraries. If ordering on vendors' forms, it is not necessary to fill out this form until the material is received. Chapter 8 provides details for processing orders that are to be cataloged for departmental libraries.

If the title is being ordered for the government documents department, searching for LC entry or card number is omitted. Succeeding steps in the ordering process are outlined below.

Figure 5.1a

CALL NO.	ORDER NO.:	AREA:	L. C. CARD NO.:	
		Engr.	77-607150	
	AUTHOR: ~~U.S. National Bureau of Standards~~			CSR
	Slattery, William J			OO
TO BE KEPT IN **Engr**	TITLE: An index of U.S. voluntary engineering standards			EDITION
LIBRARY				YEAR
PRICE **9.00**	SERIES: U.S. NBS Special publications No. 329			1971
	C13.10			VOLS.
VENDOR **GPO**	PUBLISHER	Superintendent of Documents		CAT. NO
DATE **2.6.73**		Government Printing Office		ITEM NO.
	ADDRESS	Washington, D.C. 20402		

UK LIBRARY, ACQUISITIONS DEPT. RECOMMENDATION FORM	DEPT. REQUESTING: **Engr.** APPROVED: 1.23.73 R.P.

WHEN AVAILABLE, PROVIDE INFORMATION INDICATED BY BOLD TYPE ABOVE.

NOTES TO SEARCHER:	NOTES TO ROUTER:
GPD has copy. Order copy for Engr. and have cataloged for them.	

	ENTRIES SEARCHED:	JT. AUTHS.
√ Auth. Vfd.		
√ √ Auth./Title Vfd.	___ AUTHOR	
√ √ √ Exact Copy	___ EDITOR	
E Edition Vfd.	___ CORP.	
T Trans. Vfd.	✓✓✓ TITLE	
R Reprint Vfd.		
O Not Found	___ OTHER	

Figure 5.1b

PC		NST	
INACT		ULS	
CF		CSF	
GPD		WLSP	
N&M		CSR	
IPF		SF	
MC	June 71 9963		
OTHER		OTHER	
PS		CBI	
LC		BIP	
NUC		BPR	
BM		PW	
BN		FB	
DB		PTLA	
MLC		BNB	
DA		GMP	
MCRS	71-0082 25 4B	GR	

Figure 5.2

Class No.	AUTHOR			
List Price	TITLE			
Date Ordered				
	Edition or Series			Volumes
Date Rec'd.				
	Place		Publisher	Year
Dealer				
	Recommended by		Fund Charged	Cost
No. of Copies				
Order No.				
L.C. or Wilson Card				

Executing Orders

Many governmental agencies prefer orders to be on their own order forms. Therefore, for documents department orders, the multiple copy order form is not always used. Instead, the documents department should execute ordering procedures for individual vendors. Special procedures for different vendors are described later in this chapter. The original request slip (with order slip, if used) is filed in the outstanding orders file by SuDocs number if known. If SuDocs number is unknown, then filing is by the agency's general number or by methods specified for types of publications not covered by SuDocs.

Orders Received

When the publication is received, the order slip must be pulled and carefully checked with the publication. "Received" and the date are written on the order slip. If the publication was sent from an address significantly different from the address to which the order was sent, the new address is written on the back of the order slip.

If the new publication is a serial, a subscription card with all available information is filled out and filed alphabetically in the subscriptions file.

Checking-in Procedures

Checking-in procedures for a new publication vary depending on the ultimate treatment of that item.

If the publication was requested to be uncataloged, *no* shelf list entry is made. Instead, the publication is sent directly to the person or department that ordered it.

Chapter 8 explains the methods to follow if the publication was requested to be cataloged.

Routing

Routing the new publication also depends on its ultimate destination.

If the work was ordered by the government documents section of the library, it can be shelved directly.

If it was ordered by another department, the order slip should be photocopied, and the photocopy filed in the "orders received" file and the original copy is put in the book. The book is then sent to the department that placed the order or to the cataloging department.

Problems

Problems do arise when the wrong publication is sent or when the order is incomplete.

If the book sent was not the one ordered, the vendor must be sent: 1) a copy of the order slip; 2) a description of the book sent; and 3) an explanatory note. The book cannot be sent back immediately; one must wait for a reply from the vendor.

If the order was incompletely filled, it is necessary to notify the vendor of the error and make a note on the order slip that not all items were received.

Two types of claim sheets are illustrated by Figures 5.3 and 5.4. The data shown in Figure 5.3 should be incorporated onto letterhead stationery. This style has its advantages. It allows the librarian to give detailed information concerning the order and it also facilitates the vendor's reply, since he can simply fill in the blanks. Copies may be separately typed as needed or machine reproduced. The other form (Figure 5.4) is a multiple-copy self-carbon form. Each copy in the set is color coded for easy filing and recognition.

It is a good idea to provide the exact address to which the publication was sent. This sometimes seems to be the only method an agency uses to identify its mailing list. Failure to note this address exactly often means that the library is put on another mailing list and thus begins to receive two files of the material.

SPECIAL ACQUISITIONS PROCEDURES

The procedures discussed above are general ones to follow in handling orders for government documents. However, some issuing agencies have their own forms and procedures. Libraries must follow these in order to insure maximum efficiency

Figure 5.3

The material noted above:

☒ Has not been received. Is due on our:

   X ...... Purchase subscription; standing order no. account no. 51346 ....
      ...... Exchange arrangement   ...... Complimentary subscription
      ...... Monograph order no. ....

☐ Was damaged in the mail. Please supply a perfect copy.
☐ Has not been received. Invoice no. .... has been received.
☐ Has been received. Please supply an invoice.
☐ Is no longer required. Please cancel our order or the remainder of our order.
☐ Incomplete shipment on your invoice no. ....
☐ Received .... copy. .... copy subscription.
☐ Has been received. We can find no record of an order. Please supply copy of our order.
☐ Is listed on your invoice no. .... We cannot identify. Please supply copy of our order.

Signed ....Invoice Received in Serials Division......

SPACE BELOW PROVIDED FOR YOUR REPLY. PLEASE MARK APPROPRIATE SPACE.

☐ Sent ....   ☐ On mailing list.
☐ Out of print.   ☐ Will send when reprinted (approximate date): ....
☐ Out of stock.   ☐ Searching; will send when located.
☐ Not yet published.   ☐ Approximate date of publication: ....
☐ Not published at all.
☐ Suspended with ....   Expect to resume ....
☐ Ceased publication with ....
☐ No record of ☐ Purchase subscription; standing order
              ☐ Exchange arrangement   ☐ Complimentary subscription
              ☐ Monograph order

☐ Order referred to ....
☐ Set complete in .... volumes.
☐ Remarks:

Figure 5.4

Entry: **Computer program abstracts**	Purge date: **7.11.72**

V.3, no.2   July 1971

Call No.
NAS1.44
Engr
651.805
C7395

Gov't Pub.Dept
University of Kentucky Libraries
~~Acquisitions Department~~
~~Central Serials Record~~
Lexington, Kentucky 40506

Has not been received. **on acct 51346**
Please supply on our:

☒ subscription/standing order.
☐ gift/exchange.

(PLEASE SUPPLY OR REPORT)
Thank you.

Claim
from:

⌐   **U.S. Government Printing Office**   ⌐
      Public Documents Department
      Washington, D.C. 20402

∟   ∟

Date sent: **4.11.72**   Vendor:

in the processing of their orders. The following sections of this chapter will describe forms and procedures for ordering from 1) GPO (this section also covers the selection of materials from the *Monthly Catalog*); 2) the Documents Expediting Project; 3) the National Technical Information Service; 4) the Defense Documentation Center; 5) the Atomic Energy Commission; 6) the National Aeronautics and Space Administration; and 7) Leasco, Inc., distributor of ERIC products. General rules for ordering materials appear in most of the index-abstract journals and catalogs of the government agencies. Thus, current information on prices and sources can be found in the introductory material of the appropriate index—i.e., RIE, STAR, GRA-GRI.

Requirements for depository status of individual agencies can be learned by direct inquiry. Methods of payment and price also differ for the few agencies that maintain sales programs.

Government Printing Office

The Government Printing Office assumes the responsibility of being the distributing agent for a major portion of government documents. Complete ordering instructions are given in the introductory pages of each issue of the *Monthly Catalog*. The basic procedures outlined in this manual presuppose a deposit account with the Superintendent of Documents. The routines can be followed with other methods of payment, however—by enclosing the correct amount of purchase in the form of Superintendent of Documents coupons, check, or money order.

To establish a deposit account, one sends a minimum of $25.00, in check or money order, payable to the Superintendent of Documents. The exact name and address of the individual or firm establishing the account must be clearly stated. When an account is opened, a supply of special depositor order blanks is furnished and an account number assigned. This number must be placed on all orders. The order blanks used in submitting the order are returned to the sender monthly with notations showing publications mailed, explanations regarding items not available, the amount of the charge, and the balance remaining on deposit.

To order publications on a deposit account from SuDocs, one completes a blue "deposit order blank," supplied to deposit account holders by SuDocs. The publication is identified with SuDocs number, quantity desired, title, and price. Further identification needed includes the library's deposit account number and address, the date, and the order number. The order is filed in the outstanding orders file.

After the material has been received, one follows the basic procedures for orders received. In addition, it is necessary to check the blue deposit order blank, mark "OK" by the items received, to initial and date the order blank, and to send it to bookkeeping department. If an item was not sent, it is necessary to consider reasons given and decide whether further action is necessary.

Some selections of government documents not received as depository items must be made by reading through the *Monthly Catalog*. This is done in order to assure a well-balanced collection that will serve the library's patrons adequately. Principles of selection are basically the same as those used for the library as a whole. First, it is necessary to decide whether the material fits the general subject area of the library collection; then, of course, one must ascertain whether the library already has a copy.

If the decision is made to order the publication, the procedures described below will simplify the ordering process.

1. One should make an attempt to get the publication free from one of the sources discussed in the first part of this chapter. The request for free publications may be on a postcard, as shown in Figure 5.5, or in a standard letter.

If the request is made by letter to a Congressional committee, a return address label should be included for each publication.

Regardless of the form used for the request, certain information is vital to assure satisfactory completion of the order—*viz.*, title, author, date (and any other bibliographic information necessary for identification), date mailed, signature of librarian authorized to request documents, date of *Monthly Catalog*, and return address.

2. If the publication is not available for free distribution and must be ordered from SuDocs, then one must follow the instructions for deposit account orders.

3. The fact that the item has been ordered should be noted in the *Monthly Catalog*. The simplest way to do this, as shown in Figure 5.6, is to circle the entry number in pencil (see Figure 5.6).

Figure 5.5

Government Publications Department
UNIVERSITY OF KENTUCKY LIBRARIES   7.17.72
MARGARET I. KING LIBRARY   •   LEXINGTON, KENTUCKY 40506

This library will appreciate receiving the material listed below, if it is available for free distribution. If obtainable only by purchase, please quote before sending. Thank you. *i'm. Rebekah M. Hazleton*

Nation's Stake in employment of middle-aged and older persons, working paper; ... July 1971. 1971.

(Committee print, 92d Congress, lsr session.)

Library Form No. 27
7/7/2

Figure 5.6

JULY 1972

Aeronautical and Space Sciences Committee, Senate
Washington, DC 20510

(9475) Convention on International Liability for Damage Caused by Space Objects, analysis and background data, staff report; [prepared by Daniel Hill Zafren, Legislative Attorney of American Law Division, Library of Congress]. May 1972. 1972. vi+76 p. (Committee print, 92d Congress, 2d session.)   * Paper, 35c.
L.C. card 72–602008   Y 4.Ae 8 : Sp 1/8

9476 NASA authorization for fiscal year 1973, hearings, 92d Congress, 2d session, on S. 3094.   ● Item 1032–A   Y 4.Ae 8 : N 21 a/973/pt.(nos.)
pt. 1. Mar. 14–16, 1972. 1972. xi+796 p. il.   †
        L.C. card 72–601893
pt. 2. Mar. 22–Apr. 14, 1972. 1972. vi+797–1343 p. il.   * Paper, $2.50.

Aging, Special Committee on, Senate
Washington, DC 20510

9477 Evaluation of Administration on Aging, and conduct of White House Conference on Aging, joint hearings before Special Committee on Aging and Subcommittee on Aging, 92d Congress, 2d session.
pt. 10. Feb. 3, 1972. 1972. iii+597–648 p.   * Paper, 25c.   ● Items 1009 & 1043
                                                         Y 4.Ag 4 : Ag 4/2/pt.10

9478 Nation's stake in employment of middle-aged and older persons, working paper; [prepared by staff of Senior AIDES program of National Council of Senior Citizens, Inc., Washington, D.C.] July 1971. 1971. vii+80 p. (Committee print, 92d Congress, 1st session.)   * Paper, 35c. (S/N 5270–1133).
L.C. card 72–616418   Y 4.Ag 4 : Em 7/5

4. When the material is received, the circle is erased from the *Monthly Catalog* entry number, and a check is pencilled in before the number (see Figure 5.6). Correspondence returned with the publication can then be discarded and regular checking-in procedures followed. Any outstanding order files should be cleared.

Documents Expediting Project

The Documents Expediting Project (DocEx) is the best source for obtaining many non-depository items. The Project supplies multiple request forms—one kind for monographs (Figures 5.7a and 5.7b) and one kind for serials (Figure 5.8).

1. The correct form should be typed using two carbons. The publication is identified with SuDocs number in upper left corner, agency, title, date, edition, and exact citation of bibliographic source. It is also necessary to type the correct address to which the publication should be sent, and the date of the request.

2. The first two copies are sent to:

> Documents Expediting Project
> Library of Congress
> Washington, D.C. 20540

3. The third copy is filed with SuDocs orders.

4. When the publication is received, one copy of the form will be included. The date received is noted on that copy, which is then filed with orders received. The copy in the SuDocs orders file is discarded. The basic procedures for checking in are then followed.

5. If the order slip is returned without the publication, the information on the back of the slip (see Figure 5.7a) will dictate the next step: one can re-order from the suggested source, or mark shelf list and order cards "OP" as indicated.

National Technical Information Service

The National Technical Information Service (NTIS) maintains a deposit account program similar to that of the GPO. The general rule to follow is: publications that have a PB number or an AD number from 600,000 to 700,000 are available and should be ordered from NTIS. (All other AD numbered publications should be ordered from the Defense Documentation Center, see page 69). Beginning in July 1972, NTIS initiated a single-sheet form on which more than one item may be ordered. The front of the form is to be used when report/accession number is known; the back is used when this information is not known.

1. Before ordering, decide on either microfiche or hard copy.

2. Complete the correct NTIS order form (illustrated and explained in Figure 5.9). AD publications purchased from DDC may be charged to an NTIS deposit account. The turn-around time from DDC to NTIS is minimal, so that it may often be more convenient to order from DDC direct, even though the number is in the NTIS sales sequence. Note that this form may be used even when publications are not to be charged against a deposit account. Determine first whether

Figure 5.7a

Agency: Environmental Protection Agency   EP1.2
                                             Se 8
Title: Sewage treatment plant dependability with
       special reference to activated sludge
       process.
Date: March 1971.   Edition:
Bibliographical source: Monthly Catalog January 1973,
                        no. 16032
Library: Government Publications Department
          University of Kentucky Libraries
          Lexington, Kentucky 40506
Date Requested: 11 April 1973   3

- -

☐ Publications attached
☐ Publications being sent under separate cover
☐ Publication being sent by issuing agency
☐ More information needed
☐ Publications not available at this time
☐ For sale by Superintendent of Documents
☐ For sale by issuing agency
☐ Out of print

- -

Agency: Environmental Protection Agency.   EP1.2
                                              Se 8
Title: Sewage treatment plant dependability with
        special reference to activated sludge
        process.
Date: March 1971.   Edition:
Bibliographical source: Monthly Catalog January 1973,
                        no. 16032
Library: Government Publications Department
          University of Kentucky Libraries
          Lexington, Kentucky 40506
Date Requested: 11 April 1973   1
LC 65-15 (2/59)

Figure 5.7b

```
              Government Publications Department
              University of Kentucky Libraries
              Lexington, Kentucky 40506




------------------------------------------------------------

Agency:  Environmental Protection Agency        EP1.2
                                                Se 8
Title:  Sewage treatment plant dependability with
            special reference to activated sludge
            process.
Date:   March 1971.               Edition:
Bibliographical source: Monthly Catalog January 1973,
                            no. 16032
Library: Government Publications Department
             University of Kentucky Libraries
             Lexington, Kentucky 40506
Date Requested:  11 April 1973

-------------------------------------------------------------

                                                        2

                    Order Form
                        For
          United States Government Publications
Use one slip for each title requested. The first and
second copies are to be sent to the Documents Expe-
diting Project, Library of Congress, Washington, D.C.
20540. The third copy is for the retention of the
ordering library. For orders which cannot be filled
immediately, a record will be kept in the event that
a copy can be located in the future. Notification
will be given on all orders of action taken.
```

Figure 5.8

```
    Government Publications Department
    University of Kentucky Libraries
    Lexington, Kentucky 40506




                MAIL LIST ADDITION            LC1.18
    Agency:  Library of Congress

    Title:   Library of Congress Information Bulletin

    Reference: Monthly Catalog, February 1973, no. 18578
    _____
    The Library whose mailing address appears on the
    reverse of this slip has requested that it be

        X    added to                 dropped from

    your mailing list for the publication above. Your
    cooperation will be greatly appreciated.
    65-2   (rev 9/65)
```

payment will be included, whether the order is to be shipped and billed, or whether payment is to be deducted from a deposit account. Mark the applicable space on the order form.

3. When ordering a subscription from NTIS, write a letter giving the following information: agency, title, starting volume and date, duration of subscription, and account. Mail this to:

> Department A
> National Technical Information Service
> Department of Commerce
> Springfield, Virginia 22151

Then file the request slip in the "NTIS request" file by accession/report number if known (or at the front of the file if the number is not known).

Figure 5.9

Document Number	Routing Code	Check one			Quan-tity	Unit Price	Total Price
	5	Paper Copy	Micro fiche	Other (specify)			
PB 184104	1645	x			2	3.00	6.00
Title No. 1 [4]	1646	x			1	6.00	6.00
Title No. 2	1647		x		1	0.95	0.95

Top section of form:

- ☐ Charge my NTIS deposit account no. _____ [1]
- ☐ Send me an application for an NTIS deposit account.
- ☐ Purchase order no. _____
- ☐ Check enclosed for $ _____
- ☐ Bill me (not applicable to foreign customers) add 50¢ per title.

Wherever a foreign sales price is NOT specified in the listings, all foreign buyers must add the following charges to each order.
$2.50 for each document
$1.50 for each microfiche

FOR DDC USERS ONLY [2]
DDC USER CODE _____
CONTRACT NUMBER _____
(LAST 6 CHARACTERS ONLY)

Please allow two weeks for delivery on your order. If ordering without a document number, by title only, add a week.

[3] ☐ Magnetic Tape (tape)   ☐ 7 track

☐ 200BPI
☐ 556 BPI   ☐ odd parity
☐ 800 BPI   ☐ even parity
☐ 9 track-800 BPI odd parity only

Bottom section:

Titles ordered are from: [6]
- ☐ Weekly Government Abstracts _____ titles
- ☐ NTISearch _____ titles
- ☐ Government Reports Topical Announcements _____ 2 _____ titles
- ☐ Government Reports Announcements or Index _____ titles
- ☐ Unknown Source _____ 1 _____ titles
- ☐ Other _____ titles
- _____ titles

Enter Grand Total $ 12.95 →

[1] Your Account Number.

[2] Customers ordering from Defence Documentation Service, through NTIS, must indicate their User Code and the last 6 characters of their Contract Number.

[3] If ordering Magnetic Tape fill in this information.

[4] Document Number if known, otherwise, fill in Title Number from reverse side of form.

[5] The item entered here will be shown on your shipment and on your statement with the charge for your identification purposes. (Limit 8 characters.)

[6] Indicate the number of titles and the source from which they were selected.

4. When the publication is received, follow basic procedures for checking in.

5. Make shelf list card (Figure 5.10) with AD or PB number, author, place, title, date, department that requested the publication, and whether microfiche or paper. This procedure is further explained on page 87.

Figure 5.10

```
AD 728-858   Maraschak, Jacob
             California Univ., Los Angeles.


Lib Sci   Economics of information systems. 1971.
          (micro)
```

6. Route the publication as described in "basic procedures."

Defense Documentation Center

The Defense Documentation Center (DDC) is the central distributing agency for research publications that are by or for the military.

It serves those agencies holding military or certain other kinds of contracts. This manual will describe only those procedures for acquiring unclassified materials without restricted distribution. The DDC sets forth specific procedures for establishing eligibility to order their publications and requires the completion of their order forms.

1. When ordering through DDC, complete the order form shown in Figures 5.11a and 5.11b, including contract number, user's code number, internal routing (when ordered for department other than documents), NTIS deposit account number, and AD number on the front of the form. When the AD number is not known, fill in author, title, and date on the back of the form.

2. Send the order to NTIS if it is for a document numbered from AD 600,000 to 700,000. For all other numbers, send the order to:

> Defense Documentation Center
> DDC/TSR-2
> Cameron Station
> Alexandria, Virginia 22314

Figure 5.11a

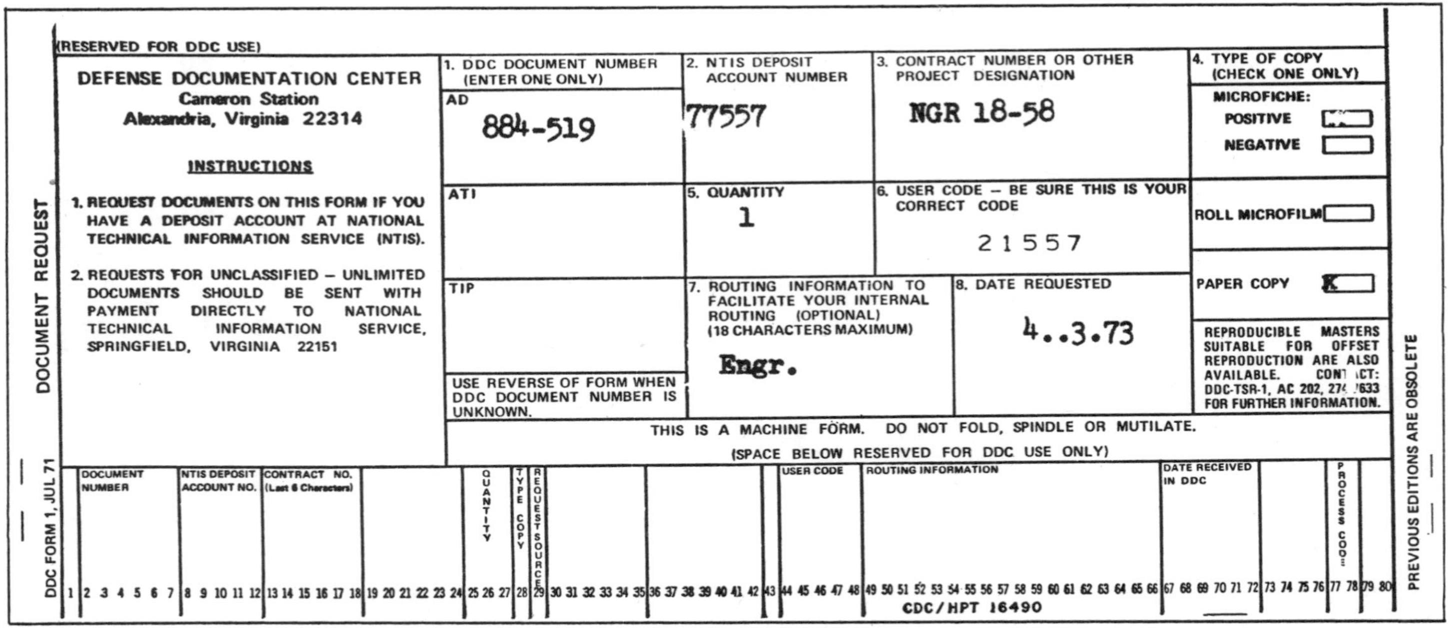

The following is the content of the DDC Document Request form (DDC Form 1, JUL 71):

DEFENSE DOCUMENTATION CENTER
Cameron Station
Alexandria, Virginia 22314

INSTRUCTIONS

1. REQUEST DOCUMENTS ON THIS FORM IF YOU HAVE A DEPOSIT ACCOUNT AT NATIONAL TECHNICAL INFORMATION SERVICE (NTIS).

2. REQUESTS FOR UNCLASSIFIED — UNLIMITED DOCUMENTS SHOULD BE SENT WITH PAYMENT DIRECTLY TO NATIONAL TECHNICAL INFORMATION SERVICE, SPRINGFIELD, VIRGINIA 22151

USE REVERSE OF FORM WHEN DDC DOCUMENT NUMBER IS UNKNOWN.

1. DDC DOCUMENT NUMBER (ENTER ONE ONLY)
AD 884-519
ATI
TIP

2. NTIS DEPOSIT ACCOUNT NUMBER
77557

3. CONTRACT NUMBER OR OTHER PROJECT DESIGNATION
NGR 18-58

4. TYPE OF COPY (CHECK ONE ONLY)
MICROFICHE:
POSITIVE ☐
NEGATIVE ☐
ROLL MICROFILM ☐
PAPER COPY ☒
REPRODUCIBLE MASTERS SUITABLE FOR OFFSET REPRODUCTION ARE ALSO AVAILABLE. CONTACT: DDC-TSR-1, AC 202, 274-6633 FOR FURTHER INFORMATION.

5. QUANTITY
1

6. USER CODE — BE SURE THIS IS YOUR CORRECT CODE
21 5 5 7

7. ROUTING INFORMATION TO FACILITATE YOUR INTERNAL ROUTING (OPTIONAL) (18 CHARACTERS MAXIMUM)
Engr.

8. DATE REQUESTED
4..3.73

THIS IS A MACHINE FORM. DO NOT FOLD, SPINDLE OR MUTILATE.

(SPACE BELOW RESERVED FOR DDC USE ONLY)

		TYPE OF COPY	SOURCE OF REPRODUCED COPY	USER CODE	ROUTING INFORMATION		DATE RECEIVED IN DDC	PROCESS CODE
DOCUMENT NUMBER	NTIS DEPOSIT ACCOUNT NO.	CONTRACT NO. (Last 6 Characters)						

1 2 3 4 5 6 7 | 8 9 10 11 12 | 13 14 15 16 17 18 | 19 20 21 22 23 24 | 25 26 27 28 | 29 | 30 31 32 33 34 | 35 36 37 38 39 40 41 42 | 43 | 44 45 46 47 | 48 49 | 50 51 52 53 54 55 56 57 58 59 60 61 62 63 64 65 66 | 67 68 69 70 71 | 72 | 73 74 75 76 | 77 78 | 79 80

CDC / HPT 16490

DDC FORM 1, JUL 71

(RESERVED FOR DDC USE)

PREVIOUS EDITIONS ARE OBSOLETE

DOCUMENT REQUEST

Figure 5.11b

WHEN DDC DOCUMENT NUMBER IS UNKNOWN, PRINT OR TYPE:	(RESERVED FOR DDC USE)	
A. ALL IDENTIFYING INFORMATION B. YOUR COMPLETE MAILING ADDRESS IN BLOCK NO. 5		
1. SPONSORING MILITARY ACTIVITY	2. MILITARY SERIES NUMBER	3. ORIGINATING ACTIVITY (GIVE SPECIFIC LABORATORY OR DIVISION AND LOCATION)
Army Materiel Command **Washington, D.C.**		
4. ORIGINATOR'S SERIES NUMBER	5. COMPLETE MAILING ADDRESS OF REQUESTING ORGANIZATION	6. PERIOD COVERED AND/OR PROGRESS REPORT NUMBER
7. PROJECT NUMBER	Government Publications Department University of Kentucky Library Lexington, Kentucky 40506	
8. CONTRACT OR GRANT NUMBER OF REPORT		9. DATE PUBLISHED
		1971
10. REPORT TITLE AND PERSONAL AUTHORS Wilson, D.R. Engineering design handbook, hydraulic fliuds.		

CDC/HPT 16490B

3. File request slip with NTIS order.

4. When the publication has been received, follow basic procedures for checking in and type shelf list as indicated for NTIS items on page 87.

Atomic Energy Commission

For many years, the Atomic Energy Commission (AEC) maintained a network of depository libraries. Research literature generated by universities, private laboratories, and government installations was distributed in book form. Much research from foreign sources was distributed through USAEC. In 1962, the volume of material forced a change in publication policy. Microcards, and later microfiche, were distributed. The sales arm of the Commission then held only temporarily a stock of printed materials; it now maintains a microformat inventory. There is no information on a depository as such, but previously designated institutions still receive informational materials as before. The designation "Dep." is still given in the availability section of *Nuclear Science Abstracts* because most of the former depositories continued their collections by subscribing to commercial services.

When funds for AEC were diminished, the Commission could no longer maintain its policy of supplying free microfiche. It now contracts with commercial firms to sell the reports either in the form of microfiche or as hard copy.

Most distributors prefer a deposit account but will accept individual orders. Institutions have the option of buying the entire output or of selecting certain subject categories.

A standard order form may be used to request a title from AEC's Division of Technical Information Extension (see Figures 5.12a and 5.12b). If they have a full-size copy in stock, they will supply this form, especially for current reports. If copy is not available, they will route to the publications contractor or stop the order, as requested by the library (see Figure 5.12b).

If an older report is needed, then the order should be directed to the issuing organization. Contractors and prices change, so no attempt is made here to delineate specifics. In general, there is a standard price for microformat and a sliding scale for paper copy, depending upon size and date of publication.

Basic ordering and checking procedures are followed. If the material replaces a missing item or completes a faulty title, the checking card needs to show only that the entire title is now in the library.

National Aeronautics and Space Administration

The National Aeronautics and Space Administration (NASA) maintains depository collections in libraries and other institutions. The agency supplies hard copies of a number of series, but most of their publications come in the form of microfiche.

NASA has used various methods of indicating what the depository institution should receive. The latest, and apparently the permanent method, is to use its abstract journal *STAR (Scientific and Technical Aerospace Reports)* to indicate the items available, by means of an asterisk and number sign–i.e., *#.

Figure 5.12a

(Staple and Submit in Duplicate to DTI Extension)

TI-114 (11-63)	DEPOSITORY LIBRARY REQUEST			(For DTIE use only)
Report Number (One report per request form)		Copies	Request Date	We have

Title (Give sufficient information to properly identify report)

We have
- [ ] No copy
- [ ] Microcard copy

Please send
- [ ] Full size copy
- [ ] Microcopy

Copies Available
Yes [ ] No [ ]

Authors

Originating Organization

Report Date	Contract No. of Report	Source of Reference

Requested for

Signature

DTIE ACTION (Do not write in this space)

1. DTIE has master copy   Yes [ ] No [ ]

2. Report has been
   Microcopied MC   MN   Yes [ ] No [ ]

3. Send requester
   - a. Microcards----------- [ ]
   - b. Eye-legible copy------ [ ]
   - c. Facsimile copy-------- [ ]

(Enter your complete mailing address below and return to DTI Extension)

From: U. S. Atomic Energy Commission
Division of Technical Information Extension
P. O. Box 62
Oak Ridge, Tennessee 37830

⌜To

NOTE: DTIE will not furnish full size copies of those reports which you received in Micronegative form.

Figure 5.12b

☐ 1. We have no information concerning the release of this report. We will inquire of the issuing organization and inform you of the report's availability as soon as we have that information.

☐ 2. Not yet available. You will receive the report automatically when distribution is made.

☐ 3. Report has been published in _____.

☐ 4. Cannot be identified from the information furnished. Furnish additional information such as author, title, issuing organization, contract number and source of reference.

☐ 5. Already available to the Depository Libraries under report number

☐ 6. The requested report bears a security classification.

☐ 7. Distribution of this report has been restricted by the issuing organization. It cannot be made available to the depository libraries.

☐ 8. This report was not sponsored by the Atomic Energy Commission. We suggest you inquire of its availability from:

1. When ordering a publication that should have been received as a NASA depository item, use the form illustrated in Figure 5.13. Type all information as instructed on the back of *STAR*. File the library's copy in the outstanding orders file.

2. Items not available through the automatic distribution system may be available from the agency itself. If the order instructions in *STAR* indicate NASA as the distributor, proceed as outlined.

Items not marked with an asterisk are not NASA-generated and are not distributed free from the agency. Availability information is given at the end of the citation. If NTIS is the source, follow procedures outlined for that source. If another organization must be approached, see the appropriate acquisitions sections.

3. Send NASA orders to:

NASA Scientific and Technical Information Facility
P.O. Box 33
College Park, Maryland 20740

4. When the material has been received, the order slip is pulled from the file and the material is handled according to basic checking-in procedures on page 87.

Leasco, Inc.

The Office of Education through ERIC (Educational Resources Information Center) supplies the funds for much research which is channeled through subject clearinghouses. The results of this research are published in an endless variety of ways: house organs, articles in learned journals, parts of a series of a university or commercial publisher. The central acquisitions point is Leasco, Inc. Orders for either microfiche or hard copies must be placed through this company. The only identification they will accept is the ED number, which is the accession number assigned by the Office of Education. The procedures outlined below assume a deposit account with the distributor. Otherwise, payment accompanies the order.

1. Use the standard form provided by the vendor as shown in Figure 5.14. Send order to:

Leasco Information Products, Inc.
4827 Rugby Avenue
Bethesda, Maryland 20014

2. File request by *ED* number in outstanding orders file.
3. When publication is received, follow basic procedures for checking in (page 87).

Figure 5.13

T	R	C	CF	L	A	O	IP	R	A
U	C								

DOCUMENT REQUEST

➡ **DOCUMENT REQUESTED**

A. NASA ACCESSION NUMBER: B. NACA/NASA REPORT NUMBER

O
R

C. (PLEASE DO NOT WRITE IN THIS SPACE)

D. COPY TYPE REQUESTED   ☐ MICROFICHE   ☐ FULL SIZE

➡ **REQUESTER IDENTIFICATION**

E. REQUESTER'S FACILITY IDENT. NO. F. REQUESTER'S CONTRACT NO.

G. AUTHORIZED SIGNATURE AND DATE

NOTE: For prompt service, please follow instructions on back of last copy.

CASE FILE TO REPRO	CPRT	RPNT	PUR	NO REPRO		CF STI	GPO	OVER 200	USE MF	
				SRCE	QUAL				YES	NO

NASA SCIENTIFIC AND TECHNICAL INFORMATION FACILITY

Operated By TECHNICAL INFORMATION SERVICES COMPANY

POST OFFICE BOX 33   COLLEGE PARK, MARYLAND 20740   TELEPHONE (301) 779-2121

PLEASE TYPE

➡ **OTHER BIBLIOGRAPHIC INFORMATION** (ESSENTIAL IF ITEMS "A" AND "B" ARE UNKNOWN)

H. DOCUMENT TITLE:

I. DATE OF REPORT: J. AUTHOR(S):

K. CORPORATE SOURCE: L. CORPORATE REPORT NO.:

M. CONTRACT NO.:

N. **MAILING LABEL** (must be imprinted on all copies; include zip code)

FF 492 DEC. 68

Figure 5.14–Leasco Order Form

PURCHASE ORDER NO. GPD 11125

MATERIAL REQUESTED

ITEM	Document ED Number	Number of Copies MF	Number of Copies HC	DOCUMENT PRICE (see reverse)	TOTAL PRICE
1	066 204		1	3 29	3 29
2	066 210		3	3 29	6 58
3					
4					

HOW TO ORDER

To order ERIC REPORTS include complete information for all order form items. Please print or type all information clearly.

1. Complete "bill to" and "ship to" addresses. Be sure to complete "ship to" address if different from "bill to." A like "ship to" address may be completed as "SAME." Include zip code.

2. Order document by printing ED number in designated space. ED accession numbers are listed in Research in Education (RIE). RIE may be purchased from: Superintendent of Documents, GPO, Washington, D.C. 20402.

3. Include number of copies (1, 2, 3, etc.) to be ordered in appropriate space. Use MF space for microfiche copies, use HC space for hard copy (paper). *Check RIE for availability of document in MF and HC.*

4. Include document price from the rate schedule. (Refer to price schedule on back.) Prices published in RIE through April 1, 1971, are incorrect. Consult May 1971 and later issues for correct pricing.

5. Some ED numbers include a series of titles and will be billed by title not ED number. A list of applicable ED numbers is available.

6. Extend number of copies and document price for total price for each title.

7. Add items 1 through 15 and insert amount in "Sub-Total" box.

8. Add state sales tax for Illinois and Maryland or check box and cite tax exemption number for Illinois and Maryland only.

9. Add "Sub-Total" and "Tax" and insert amount in "Total" box.

10. Indicate payment method desired. Payment must accompany all orders of $10.00 or less.

11. SIGN AUTHORIZATION and date order.

12. Include only 15 titles per form. Complete and sign additional forms if required.

13. Quality warranty. LIPCO will replace products returned because of reproduction defects or incompleteness. The quality of the input document is not the responsibility of LIPCO. Best available copy will be supplied.

Chapter 6

PROCESSING

The main tasks in a depository collection revolve around getting publications from the mail room to the shelves. This section is basically devoted to the procedures for handling the majority of items, although there are exceptions to the general flow of materials. The routines involved are 1) sorting the mail, 2) shelf-listing all mail, 3) lettering or labeling all publications, 4) stamping all documents, 5) filing cards, and 6) shelving the publications.

SORTING THE MAIL

Depository libraries basically receive two kinds of mail: depository and non-depository (i.e., any item *not* received through the depository system). Depository mail is always distinguishable because the label contains the depository library's number in the address. This mail must be handled immediately upon its receipt in the library; there is a ten-day limit for claiming missing, incomplete, or multilated items from the Government Printing Office.

After the receipt of depository mail has been verified, the purchased and free mail must be separated. Sometimes an original order slip or copy will be returned with the item, and sometimes a packing slip or an invoice will accompany the purchased piece. Either of these facilitates identification of the item. If there is neither an order slip nor an invoice, each package must be checked before any further steps can be taken.

Purchased mail should then be handled first. It is vitally important that all records concerning money be kept accurately, and immediate completion of all steps for payment eliminates many possibilities of error. When payments have been executed, the documents can then be cataloged.

After the mail has been sorted, depository and non-depository items have been separated, and order records have been cleared, all pieces other than depository can then be divided into serials and monographs to simplify searching.

SHELF-LISTING

Because of the legal responsibilities associated with being a depository[1] and because of library accountability for materials whether purchased or free, it is necessary to keep precise records of all publications received. The routines of shelf-listing or checking in publications are vital. The integrity of the shelf list and, indeed, of the entire collection depends upon the proper handling of materials at this stage. If the shelf list cards do not reflect the exact number of the publications and the holdings on the shelves, the materials cannot be retrieved through library records. Additionally, the bibliographic control required by the Government Printing Office is lost.

Therefore, at this stage in processing, it is necessary to avoid all undue confusion, interruptions, etc.; the materials needed for the completion of all the tasks should be readily at hand.

It should be noted at this stage that libraries that do not use the Superintendent of Documents Classification System would not call this a shelf listing procedure but would call it a holdings file. As a "holdings file," however, it would still provide most of the same information and would direct the user to the actual location of the publication. If at all possible, the file should still contain the Superintendent of Documents number.

Depository Mail

Shelf-listing or checking in must be done for depository mail first, and the daily mail must be processed as it is received. Each box of depository items contains a shipping list—a record of the publications shipped. Basic steps in the checking-in process are as follows:

1. The shipping list must be dated (see Appendix C).

2. A sheet of paper with a list of shipping lists in numerical order (called a "boxes received" list) is a convenient way to determine whether materials are missing. The date is entered beside the shipping list number. For example:

Figure 6.1

S.L. No.	Date
6810	3/20/73
6811	3/20/73
6812	3/21/73
6813	3/21/73
6814	
6815	3/21/73
6816	3/22/73
6817	3/22/73

In this example it is quite apparent that a shipment is missing. Steps for claiming missing items are enumerated later in this chapter.

3. Arrange the material exactly according to the shipping list. Then check the publications received with those on the list. Mark (with a check to the left of the item number) material received. Circle the item number of material not

received. At this time examine each item to see that it is indeed the publication on the list, and note the condition of the item. More importantly, be sure that the name of the agency is the same as that on the card and that the name of the serial is the same. If a difference occurs, set aside for further investigation.

4. Find the shelf list card in the files and check in the document as shown in the examples of shelf list cards in Chapter 4. For cuttered publications, place a check card with the proper entry inside the front cover of the publication, finish the rest of the procedures, and give the publication to the typist. For numbered publications, put a check mark to the left of the number on the shelf list card that corresponds to the number of the item received. For daily, weekly, monthly, or quarterly publications, write the number of the publication in the appropriate place. For annual or semi-annual publications, check the proper date on the left hand side. *Always be sure that the numbering system used on the card matches that used on the publication.*

5. Now write the classification number on the publication (follow the routines under "lettering."

6. Separate the periodicals from the monographs, count each, and mark the numbers in the appropriate boxes on the monthly count sheets (the necessary steps and information for this are in the "counting" section later in this chapter).

7. Now stamp all publications as described in the "stamping" section below.

8. After all the documents have been checked in and processed, compare the item numbers not checked off with the "item numbers selected" sheet. This sheet is simply a listing of agencies with selected item numbers listed. It is a useful time-saver for selective depositories because a quick comparison with the shipping list will allow one to know immediately if a selected item is missing. Any missing publications must be claimed from the Government Printing Office.

9. If no publications are missing and all the above steps have been completed, mark "OK" and initial the shipping list in the upper left hand corner and file the shipping list in the completed folder. The publications are now ready to be shelved.

10. Some materials require special treatment. Instructions for these should be noted on the shelf list card. First, *be sure that the instructions are necessary.* If they are, write the instructions in pencil directly following the series title. If there is not enough space, put an asterisk after the title and write the instructions in the best clear space. Be concise but clear in the wording of the instructions—e.g., "shelve with _____," or "claimed" and date. Erase the instructions as soon as they are no longer necessary. If the instructions become a permanent part of the procedures, type them on the card.

Some examples of special instructions follow. If the series is renumbered by year, or by appearance, the date is usually the second line of the classification, and the book number is the third line. All issues of this type of series should be retained, and, therefore, instructions are provided as shown below:

FS5.3	FS5.3	U.S. Education Office.
1956	1957	Bulletin
no.--	no.--	

Keep all issues.

If the series is numbered continuously, the item may be a revision (as in the first example below) or a subseries (as in the second example) with the same number for each issue. The book number is the second line, and the date is the third line.

Example:

FS5.4	FS5.4	U.S. Education Office
no. 486	no. 486	State provisions for
	1961	school bus insurance.

Discard earlier edition.

Example:

Al.34	Al.34	U.S. Agriculture Department.
no. 233	no.233	Change in farm produc-
	1972	tion and efficiency.

Keep all. Each issue covers a different time.

In general, determine from the book itself into which category the material falls, and then decide whether to discard (revision) or retain (series). Write in upper right hand corner of the publication: "Discard either edition" or "Keep all issues."

Problems with Depository Mail

Problems occur with enough regularity that they can be categorized. Generally these problems are: 1) items missing from a shipment; 2) items marked "shipped separately"; 3) "do not claim" cards sent with shipment in lieu of the item; 4) defective copies of publications; 5) shipment arrives without a shipping list; and 6) missing shipment.

1. For missing items, complete a depository claim form (Figure 6.2) giving all information required and send the form to:

> Library
> Public Documents Department
> United States Government Printing Office
> Washington, D.C. 20402

Note the date claimed on the shipping list, circle the item number, and file it with incomplete shipping lists when the remainder of the shipment is processed.

When the publication arrives, pull the shipping list out of the incomplete file and erase the circle around the item number. Make a check mark to the left of the item number, and proceed with regular check-in steps.

If the Superintendent of Documents replies that the publication is no longer available, pull the shipping list out of the incomplete file, and write "not available" next to the item number. Pull the shelf list card and note on the card that the

Figure 6.2

UNITED STATES GOVERNMENT PRINTING OFFICE

PUBLIC DOCUMENTS DEPARTMENT

WASHINGTON, D.C.   20402

CLAIM FOR DEPOSITORY PUBLICATIONS SELECTED BUT NOT RECEIVED

(For Use with Daily Depository Shipping Lists)

All claims for nonreceipt of depository publications must be postmarked within 10 days from the date of receipt of the issue of the Daily Depository Shipping List concerned. False statement on this application is punishable by law (U.S. Code, Title 18, Section 287).

Mail claims to: Library
Public Documents Department
U.S. Government Printing Office
Washington, D.C.   20402

I certify that this depository did not receive the following items listed in the Daily Depository Shipping List, No. **6833** dated ....**March 30, 1973**........ although they were selected in advance by this depository. This issue of the Daily Depository Shipping List was received by the depository on ....**April 5, 1973**..........

Signature of librarian authorized to make claim on behalf of depository *Mar. Rbleld, M. Horlston*

Depository Library No. ....**208**............................   Date........**March 5, 1973**.

Item	Title	Classification
....**324**........	**FM 5136 (Reprint includes chg.1)** **Oct.1970**	**D101.20:5-136**

publication is not available. Then mark the shipping list "OK," initial in the upper left corner, and file with completed shipping lists.

2. Items marked "shipped separately" often require no special handling. If piece has been received, follow regular procedure. If piece has not been received, file shipping list with incomplete ones. Allow ten days to two weeks for receipt, and claim according to procedure outlined above. When the missing publication arrives, pull the shipping list from incomplete file, erase the circle, check, and then follow normal check-in procedure. Mark shipping list "OK," initial, and file with completed shipping lists.

3. "Do Not Claim" cards are sent when the press run of a publication has been insufficient to supply a copy to each depository. A sample is shown in Figure 6.3. Circle the item number of the missing publication on the shipping list, and fasten the card to it.

Figure 6.3

```
                    IMPORTANT

DUE TO SHORTAGE OF STOCK THIS PUBLICATION WAS OMITTED
FROM YOUR PACKAGE FOR THE INDICATED LIST. IT WILL BE
MAILED TO YOU AS SOON AS AVAILABLE. DO NOT MAKE CLAIM
FOR THIS PUBLICATION.

        Shipping List 5960      Item 507-B-5
        2nd Shipment 5/17/71
        Research & Education: Top Priorities
        For Mentally Ill Children ETC.Confer
        ence June 24-27,1970 San Francisco
        Ca.,
```

After following regular check-in routines for all the publications on the shipping list, circle the item number of the missing publication and clip the "Do Not Claim" card to it. File the shipping list in the incomplete file.

If the publication arrives, pull the shipping list and erase the circle around the item number, and follow all check-in procedures.

If the publication is not received within two months, mark "not received" by the item, date, and file shipping list in completed folder.

4. Defective Items: Include those with paper material that is badly torn or rumpled, any bound volume with spine badly broken, any material that has unaccounted-for blank pages, and any items with illegible printing.

Send a regular depository claim form, adding in bold type the word *defective*. Hold defective copy for instructions from the Superintendent of Documents.

When replacement copy arrives, check-in in the regular manner. Dispose of or return defective material as directed by the Superintendent of Documents.

5. For shipments with a missing shipping list, clip a note saying "shipping list missing/date" to the top item in the package and hold. Request from the regional library—or a neighboring library—the number or a copy of the list, giving titles of some of the documents, or send a regular depository claim form to the Superintendent of Documents for a copy of the list. When the shipping list is received, follow regular procedure.

6. Missing Boxes: If a date does not appear beside the shipping list number on the "Boxes Received" form (Figure 6.1), and there are no boxes without shipping lists, send a regular depository claim form to the Superintendent of Documents after allowing approximately ten days to two weeks for receipt of box. When box is received, follow prescribed procedure.

Special Processes

1. Survey sheets are sent out periodically. They announce new series and include sample-issues and item number cards that must be handled immediately if the library wishes to receive the series. Therefore, it is first necessary to be sure that all item number cards and samples are included and to claim any missing cards or samples from GPO.

Complete depositories will automatically return a copy of each item number card; regional libraries will keep one copy but need not return one to SuDocs.

Selective depositories will have to chose the ones that it wishes to receive. Then separate the cards for the series selected from the cards for the series not selected. (If any card had to be claimed, write the number on a 3" x 5" card with date claimed.) File both cards for series not selected in the items not received file. For selected titles, type in the lower left corner, on one item number card, the date selected. This position separates the date from all other information on card and eliminates possible confusion. On the second card, stamp the depository library number and mail card to:

> Library
> P.O. Box 1533
> Washington, D. C. 20013

The item numbers of the new series should then be added to the "item numbers selected" sheet.

2. Selective depositories should mark each new annual issue of the *List of Classes of United States Government Publications Available*. It is important to check the publications being currently received. This will give the library a quick reference source and will avoid the need for checking the item number for the series.

Check the list against the "item number received" file to be sure that all series received are marked. (This procedure can be done while checking changes made by the Superintendent of Documents.)

File the old edition. This can be used in checking the history of a series or agency. Keep the new revised edition available for reference use.

3. Sometimes new series are added or classification numbers are changed without any notice on the shipping list. When this occurs, pull the item number card and clip it to the publication. Finish the rest of the check-in procedures. See also Chapter 7, "Specialized Procedures," for a section on changes in documents number.

4. New shelf list cards for serials should be made when the space on the old card is filled. At that time, check in the publication, clip a new card to the old one, and follow the rest of the check-in procedures. Then copy the correct entry from the old card to the new one and re-file.

Publications Requiring Special Treatment

Certain types of publications require somewhat different treatment when they are being checked in. Examples and procedures follow.

1. *Cumulated Editions:* (Some examples are *Supreme Court Reports* or *Statutes at Large*.) Check in according to standard procedures. Then mark original shelf list card "withdrawn" and attach note describing superseded issues to be discarded. If original material was counted, mark the number of items withdrawn.

2. *Revisions:* Check in revisions according to all basic routines. Write on publication in upper right corner "Discard earlier edition," unless the card indicates that a decision has been made to keep all editions. Mark one copy "withdrawn" on the monthly statistics sheet, if applicable.

3. *Transmittals or Errata Sheets* (corrections or updates for an established volume): Check these off on the shipping list, then write the classification number in the upper left corner of the transmittal or errata sheet. Make records only of pieces that will stand alone on the shelf. Stamp these and insert or make corrections at less busy times.

4. *Bills, Resolutions:* (These can be handled by standard procedure or in the following manner.) Do not check in and do not stamp until circulated. Maintain a separate count for these, so that statistics will not be out of balance. Always add to "number of documents handled" record. Shelve by Congress, Session, Chamber, series and number.

5. *Documents and Reports:* Do not check in, letter, or stamp. Arrange on the shelf by Congress, Session, Chamber, series (i.e., document or report), and number. Count and add to the "number of documents handled" record.

6. *Serial Set:* In *Numerical List and Schedule of Volumes*, check the volume and date received. If the volume is not yet listed, clip a paper inside the last issue giving Congress, Session, Chamber, series number (i.e., document or report, and number), serial number (i.e., serial set number as indicated on spine), and date received. On regular numbered cards, check volume received to give a complete, easily consulted record of holdings.

7. *Hearings:* (These can be handled by standard procedure or in the following manner.) If the library maintains a complete collection, shelve by Congress, Session, Chamber, committee, and title. There is no need to maintain holdings records for a

complete collection. If the collection is incomplete, shelve by Superintendent of Documents number and make shelf list card according to regular procedures.

Exceptions in the Daily Depository Mail

The following material is mailed daily. Although it is depository material, it is not listed on depository shipping lists. It is checked, and any missing items are claimed just like other depository mail.

> *Federal Register*
> Daily edition of *Congressional Record*
> *Daily Statement of Treasury*
> *News Digest*, Securities and Exchange Commission
> *Senate Calendar*
> *House Calendar*
> *Weekly Compilation of Presidential Documents*

Find the classification number in the subscription listing of the February *Monthly Catalog* and check in according to regular procedures. Claim any missing issues immediately on a regular depository claim form from GPO. When the claimed piece is received, check in according to regular procedures.

Non-Depository Mail

Preliminary Procedures

Clear all acquisitions records and remove all publications with already established classification numbers. Proceed with detailed procedures for these. Separate all unidentified publications into serials and monographs. Hold the material to establish the correct classification number and where necessary, the correct entry. (See detailed procedures in Chapter 7.) Check in on shelf list when properly identified.

Detailed Procedures

Find the shelf list card in the files and check in the document as shown previously. For cuttered publications, place a check card with the proper entry inside the front cover of the publication, finish the rest of the procedures, and give the publication to the typist. For numbered publications, put a check mark on the left of the number that was received. For daily, weekly, monthly, or quarterly publications, write the number of the publication in the appropriate place. For annual or semi-annual publications, check the proper date on the left hand side. *Always be sure that the numbering system used on the card matches that used on the publication.* Now follow procedures 4 through 10 under depository mail.

Exceptions

1. Missing issues of periodicals (back issues not checked off): Go to the shelves to be sure the publication has not been received. Send a claim form to the supplier (see Chapter 5 for examples) using address from order slip or subscription file, or from the latest issue received, describing the missing item, order number, and address of subscriber. Place an asterisk where the missing issue would be checked in and write in pencil on the bottom of the card "claimed/date."

2. Publications never listed in the *Monthly Catalog*: For monographs (see Figure 6.4), find the class stem number that most closely fits the publication. From a two-figure Cutter table, determine the Cutter number for the piece. Add a raised zero (^{o}) to the Cutter number to indicate that this number is assumed. Type cards (author, title, and shelf list) and indicate the date the series was cataloged. For serials, find the class stem number that most closely fits the publication. Assign a series number that would be higher than any anticipated by the agency, and type cards (author, title, and shelf list). Indicate the date series was cataloged. For a detailed description of how to create class numbers see page 103.

3. Quasi-documents (ERIC materials, government technical reports, NASA depository, AEC subscriptions, etc.) in microfiche and printed forms: Microformat materials should be arranged according to the accession number assigned by the issuing agency. The materials are then counted according to the steps described in the counting section of this chapter and the number is entered on the monthly statistical sheet. It is necessary to establish control procedures. Some libraries maintain that control somewhere is essential. Others assume that holdings of complete subscriptions may be assumed and claimed only as need is discovered.

Photocopies or printed materials are arranged by funding department and then by accession or contract number assigned to the study. These materials are then entered on shelf list cards. The accession number is placed in the call number area. The funding agency is listed in the author area, and the personal author, title, and date are listed two lines below the author. These materials are now lettered in the upper left hand corner with the accession number. All materials are counted as monographs and listed on the monthly statistics sheet. Stamp these publications and shelve them separately from the rest of the collection.

LETTERING OR LABELING

After the documents have been checked in, they must be properly lettered so that they may be stored and retrieved with speed and convenience. Efficiency in this area requires that the location of the documents number be standardized, so that it may be found at a glance. Therefore, the following method for breaking the number down into concise logical units has been developed. This method for writing the documents number allows the number to be read and understood quickly. The manner in which this number is written also determines the ease with which the publication may be found. In the *Monthly Catalog*, shipping lists, and other indexing media, the document numbers are usually written on one line so as to use less space and facilitate the printing process; however, this method is cumbersome to use in a library because labels and book spines are seldom wide enough for the

Figure 6.4

```
      16
Y3.F31    U.S.  Federal  Council  for  Science  and
  2                 Technology.
              General  publications.
      0
In3           Toward  a  national  information  system,
          progress  of  the  U.S.  government  in
          scientific  and  technical  communications.
          1965.  (cat.  6.18.68)
```

number. Also, patrons and library staff find it difficult to distinguish the numbers when all parts appear on the same line. Because the eye span of most people is not wide, the vertical lettering system is easier to read.

Position

In general, all paperbound materials should have the classification number written in pencil in the upper left hand corner of the cover. All bound (hardcover) materials should have the document number on the first page or the verso (back side) of the title page, and on the spine one-inch from the bottom of the book. Exceptions are as follows: If essential words exist in the area to be marked, do not cover them, but place the classification number as close as possible to its proper place. If the paper is too dark for pencil, place a white gummed label in the proper area and then write the classification number. Also, write the call number on the first page or on the verso of the title page. If the spine is too small, place the number on the front cover an inch from the bottom of the book flush with the spine.

Format

The first and most important thing to remember is to check in the document before lettering.

If you have to stop in the process of checking in the item, you will have its receipt noted on the shelf list. If it is not lettered, it can not be shelved. But if you letter before you mark the shelf list, and are interrupted, then the publication could reach the shelf before it is recorded.

General Rules

When the slash or shilling mark appears before the colon, it *always* means raise the number or letter following it. The colon *always* means to drop the number following it to the next line. A slash mark following a colon may mean raise or drop the following number. (The meaning of the letters and numbers following the colon can sometimes be determined only by looking at the publication itself or by checking other publications in the series.)

Examples:

A1.38/2:800 will be written A1.38^2
no. 800

A1.96:966 will be written A1.96
1966

C42.8:75/32 will be written C43.8
v. 75
no. 32

Y4.Ec7:Ec7/2 will be written Y4.Ec7
Ec7^2

Abbreviations

v. stands for volume; no. stands for number; pt. stands for part; supp. stands for supplement; c. stands for copy; add. stands for addendum; trans. stands for transmittal.

STAMPING PROCEDURES

Depository materials are usually stamped in several places with the name of the library, to establish ownership easily. Since documents are a part of the total library collection, they should also be stamped in accordance with general library practice; however, to help distinguish depository from non-depository materials and to facilitate the weeding of the collection, a dated depository stamp should be used on all depository materials received. This stamp will make it unnecessary to distinguish depository materials from non-depository materials on the shelf list cards. Use of the stamp will make it easy to tell whether, and when, an item may be discarded. Also, the dated depository stamp makes it possible to check back to the shipping list if a question arises about a particular publication.

An optional stamp for use with the collection of non-depository material would be a dated documents stamp. This would distinguish documents from the rest of the collection and would help the librarian establish projected arrival dates of regularly issued materials such as annual publications. Using this stamp, the librarian could check the date of the last publication received in a series and could inform patrons of the probable availability of the next publication.

KEEPING STATISTICAL RECORDS

In its *Higher Education General Information Survey: Library Collection, Staff, Expenditures, and Salaries,* the United States Office of Education states, "depository libraries should ordinarily include in their total count documents classified in accordance with the Superintendent of Documents Classification."[2] This means that the government publication should be counted not only for departmental records but also for the records of the library as a whole. To do this, monographs (publications that are cuttered, issued annually or semi-annually, or numbered continuously), periodicals (publications which do not meet the definition of a monograph should be counted in the periodical column, i.e., transmittals, bills, preprints, and materials to be superseded by cumulative volumes), and microformat materials must be counted and recorded separately in departmental statistics.

Recording monographs and microformat materials is a fairly straightforward procedure; however, the recording of periodicals presents some special problems. The United States Office of Education directs libraries to include in their total count for printed material only *bound* periodical volumes. However, most libraries like to maintain a record of the total number of items processed by departments for the purpose of establishing work load, staff needs, etc. In order to accomplish both aims, the number of periodicals received monthly by the library must then be recorded on the monthly statistics sheet (see Figure 6.5), while the number of periodical volumes bound each year may be determined by checking the binding sheet for that year.

At the end of the year, the number of *volumes added* to the collection will be the total of the number of monographs received plus the number of periodical volumes bound. The number of *items handled* during the year will be determined by adding the number of monographs received to the number of periodicals and microforms received.

To determine the total number of volumes in the collection, the volumes recorded for the current year should be added to the total volumes in the collection, and the number of publications withdrawn should be subtracted.

In general, the following procedures should be followed. Separate the publications according to their forms (i.e., monographs or periodical). Count the monographs and enter their number on the monthly statistics sheet. Count the periodicals and enter this number on the monthly statistics sheet.

For periodicals, special instructions should be followed. At the end of the fiscal year, check the binding records for the year. Count each physical unit of periodical materials bound as one volume. Add this number to the total number of monographs received for the number of volumes added. Do not count material to be superseded by bound volumes or by microfilm such as *Daily Congressional Record, Minerals Yearbook* preprints, Supreme Court preprints, slip laws, *Federal Register,* or *Official Gazette.* At the end of the year, count as one volume all daily pieces of *Daily Treasury Statement, S.E.C. Newsletter,* and House and Senate calendars. Do not add bills. Put number on statistics sheet and circle to separate.

Figure 6.5

MONTHLY STATISTICS SHEET

Month _____

DAYS	MONOGRAPHS	PERIODICALS	MICROFILM	MICROFICHE	WITHDRAWN
1					
2					
3					
4					
5					
6					
7					
8					
9					
10					
11					

For microforms, count microfilm by the reel and microfiche, microcard, and microprint by the following formulae:

> Microfilm—number of reels
> Microprint—91 cards to the inch
> Microcard—65 cards to the inch
> Microfiche—93 cards to the inch without envelopes
> Microfiche—75 cards to the inch with envelopes

FILING

Filing rules and procedures for the government documents department vary according to the type of files kept. Chapter 4 describes types and forms of records that should be kept. The following instructions show how these files can best be maintained.

Order File

These cards are filed by Superintendent of Documents Classification Number if known. If the classification number is unknown, file by the first part of the assumed call number at the beginning of that section. Orders for hearings should be filed first by House, then committee, Congress, and Session. Senate hearings are filed in the same manner. Orders for Serial set preliminary issues are filed by Chamber, then document or report, Congress, and Session.

Exceptions are materials ordered from NTIS, ERIC, etc., which should be filed by accession number.

An alternate procedure for the order file is to arrange all orders alphabetically by main entry.

Shelf List File

These cards will be filed in alpha-numerical order by their document numbers.

Item Number Cards

These are filed in strict numerical order. If there are more than one series to an item number as a result of different series, put the original card first, followed by the others in order of SuDocs Classification Number. If there are more than one series to an item number because of a change in identification of that series, put the current one in front and the others in chronological order.

Author and Series Title Files

File these cards alphabetically word by word.[3]

Correct order	Incorrect order
New Amsterdam	New Amsterdam
New England	Newark
New wives for old	New England
Newark	Newman
Newman	New wives for old

Do not file by *a*, *an*, or *the* if it is the initial word in a title. File abbreviations as if they were spelled out in full. Disregard punctuation marks and apostrophes (i.e., *women's* would be filed *womens*).

Subscription File

The subscription file seems best arranged alphabetically by title of the series. This is the most significant element in the acquisition and it is generally what the searcher asks about. Other information is secondary. If the title of the series changes, adequate cross reference should be made in the subscription file as in all other records.

Bound Volume Status File

This is in shelf list order according to document number.

SHELVING

Basic to the use of any collection is the ability to retrieve publications from the shelves with speed and ease. To accomplish this aim, publications must be arranged on the shelves in their correct classification number order, and should be accessible through the use of the *Monthly Catalog*.

Although it is not always useful to maintain the strict arrangement of publications by their documents number—and indeed, many libraries have found it helpful to keep some items like the *Monthly Catalog* near the librarian's desk—it is essential to remember that every exception made in arranging materials on the shelves will render the *Monthly Catalog* a little less useful and will require more time to locate the actual materials.

The following rules and procedures have been developed to insure that documents will be arranged correctly and be easily retrieved.

General Procedures

Publications on the shelves should be arranged in exactly the same order as the cards in the shelf list unless clear cross references are made on the cards and the shelves. Letters are filed before numbers. File first by the letter or letters at the beginning of the classification number. File next by the whole number up to the period. Then file by the whole number up to the separation mark (i.e., the slash mark or the colon). Continue filing by the whole number or letters up to the next punctuation mark or line. *Remember that if the filing sequence demands a choice between a numeral or a letter, the letters take precedence* (e.g., FS 3.64: R4 would precede FS 3.64:46). Also, years, as part of the number, take precedence over series numbers. See sample arrangement below.

A Sample Arrangement:

> Y4.Ec7
> Ec7
>
> Y4.Ec7
> Ec7
> 1967
>
> Y4.Ec7
> Ec7^2
>
> Y4.Ec7
> Ec7a
>
> Y4.Ec7
> Ec7a
> 1967
>
> Yr.Ec7
> Ec7a^4
>
> Y4.Ec7
> no. 88
>
> Y4.Ec7^2

Exceptions

The most common exceptions are discussed below. Publications shelved out of their normal places are usually reference tools, oversized items, or those with a change in classification number. For reference tools such as the *Monthly Catalog* or the *Monthly Checklist of State Publications*, place a dummy on the shelves with a note directing the patron to the proper location of the materials. Note the location of the material in pencil on the check card.

Change in classification number occurs when materials have been moved to a new number to keep them in one place in the collection. In this case, place a dummy on the shelves with cross references directing the patron to the new location. Note on the check card the location of the materials.

Oversize items are those that are too tall to fit in normal stacks. Place a dummy on the shelves with a note directing the patron to the proper location of the materials. Note in pencil on the check card the location of the material. For certain kinds of oversized materials, it is sometimes helpful to post a listing of the materials in a prominent place.

Publications that are duplicates of items already on the shelf are handled differently. First be sure that it is an exact copy. If the newer item is not marked "C.2," "C.3," etc., write "dup." in pencil in the upper right hand corner. Place the material on the duplicate shelf (the librarian will either withdraw the publication or add it as a copy as is deemed necessary).

For revisions, check to make sure which item is the latest. Remove the earlier edition and write "old edition" in pencil in the upper right hand corner. Place the material on the duplicate shelf. (Since this material has already been withdrawn in the statistics, it may be checked and discarded by the librarian.)

Transmittals and errata sheets also require special handling. The basic volume should be pulled from the shelves. The transmittal pages or errata changes should then be substituted as directed into the publications, tipped into the publication, or written in pencil as directed. If the basic volume is not on the shelf, return the correction to the work area. Note "missing/date" on the check card and order a replacement.

An optional method for bills, documents, and reports is to shelve them by Congress, Session, series, and number. Discard original edition when "Star Print" (*) is received (a corrected version of a Congressional publication). The alternative to this is to shelve all versions of a bill together.

If the library maintains a complete collection of hearings, shelve them by Congress, Session, Chamber, committee, and title. If the collection is incomplete, shelve by the Superintendent of Documents Classification number.

Serial sets are shelved by serial number.

Shelf Reading

An important but often disliked aspect of shelving documents is shelf reading. This must be done both carefully and often, since misshelved publications are lost publications.

Each worker (student aide) is assigned a section of shelves to read. Each section of shelves should be completely read every two weeks. Questionable items—i.e., duplicates or old editions—should be brought to the attention of the librarian. A notation should be made as to where the reading left off the previous time, and this should be the starting point of the next reading. Areas that need special attention will be marked on the "Attention Sheet" (Figure 6.8) and these should be looked after immediately.

Figure 6.8

_____: Attention needed on these Ranges/
and Sections

DOCUMENTS NEED:
    aligning with shelves _____
    book ends   _____
    boxes   _____
    other*   *Ranges*_____

BOXES NEED: *Ranges 31A, Sections 4 to 7*
    dusting   _____
    dividing (too full)   _____
    labeling   _____
    turning labels to view_____
    replacing with new boxes and labeling *15B, Sections*
          5,6,7, 14A, Section 2

SHELVES NEED:
    shifting to allow depth_____
    shifting to save space_____

    *Directed activities as needed:
        Library stamping: 3 sides

INVENTORY

It seems inevitable that libraries will lose some books. Some are lost, some stolen, and some perhaps hopelessly misshelved.

Because government documents are printed in limited numbers and rapidly become difficult or impossible to replace, it is imperative that immediate steps be taken to replace missing or worn books.

Shelf reading may reveal missing items as readers notice gaps in series that are sequential (year, month, volume, or number). Generally, the loss of a monograph is noticed only when a specific request is made for it.

A systematic inventory must be made to determine which books need to be replaced. Some libraries devote a single day to the procedure of taking stock of what is in the collection. The library is closed, and all staff and student assistants report for duty.

A more effective method might be a continuing inventory, which investigates sections of shelving or the publications of an agency, one at a time. A rotation schedule could then allow for an area to be checked at least once a year (or more often if necessary).

If the worker feels that he spends more time filling out records than he does in actually performing his duties, this multiplicity of forms can set up a psychological barrier. Nevertheless, certain procedures must be standardized in order that the functions of the library can be carried out with little disruption. A report on missing books is needed so that the librarian can decide what actions will be taken. Figures 6.9a and 6.9b are examples of the forms used to report missing books.

Figure 6.9a

```
┌────────────────────────────────────────────────────────────┐
│                                                            │
│                   Missing_____             │
│                             date                           │
│                                                            │
│                                                            │
│   _____         │
│   Class number                                             │
│                                                            │
│   _____         │
│   Title in full for order purposes                         │
│                                                            │
│                                                            │
│   _____         │
│   RESULTS OF SEARCHING - over                              │
└────────────────────────────────────────────────────────────┘
```

Figure 6.9b

```
┌────────────────────────────────────────────────────────────┐
│                                                            │
│   Searches:      First           Second                    │
│      Dates:      -------          _____          │
│                                                            │
│   Initials:      _____         _____          │
│                                                            │
│   RESULTS: (Please check)                                  │
│       Found:     _____         _____          │
│   NOT FOUND:     _____         _____          │
│                                                            │
│   REPLACEMENT ORDERED?  _____        │
│                                                            │
│                                                            │
└────────────────────────────────────────────────────────────┘
```

Identify the missing document on the form. Assign searching twice, by two different people, over a specified period of time. Consider the document missing and mark the holdings record. If the decision is made to replace it, follow regular procedures for acquisitions and holdings cards. Stamp "non-depository" if replacing a non-depository item, or "depository" if replacing a depository item.

FOOTNOTES

[1] U.S. Superintendent of Documents. *Instructions to Depository Libraries.* Washington, D.C., Government Printing Office, 1967, p. 5.

[2] U.S. Office of Education. "Higher Education General Information Survey: Library Collection, Staff, Expenditures, and Salaries," in *Library Statistics of Colleges and Universities, Analytic Reports, Fall 1968.* Washington, GPO, 1970, pp. 72-82.

[3] Sophie Hiss. *ALA Rules for Filing Catalog Cards,* (Chicago, American Association, 1942).

Chapter 7

SPECIALIZED PROCEDURES

The preceding chapters have discussed the nature of the documents collection, explaining the need for special handling of government generated materials. Generalizations allow for individual approaches to the various stages of technical processes, and specific methods have been provided to serve as examples to the uninitiated and as refreshers to the seasoned librarian. Later chapters will discuss some of the "housekeeping" chores that are performed by the staff.

This chapter concerns itself with the detailed functioning of the government and its agencies, and with the output of these agencies. When there are no complications, the handling of the documents is fairly routine, and most of the steps outlined could be performed by well-trained support staff. We have now reached the point, however, at which the ingenuity of the cataloger is taxed. The real test of the detective ability and perseverance of the librarian comes with the tracing of the many convolutions of agencies and series.

Without exact cataloging and classifying (whether by Superintendent of Documents, LC, or other systems) reference service would falter. It is this precise identification that allows for efficient retrieval of the document and its information.

CORRECTIONS

Each year the agencies of the federal government print thousands of items that must be classified, listed in the *Monthly Catalog*, and distributed to depository libraries by the Superintendent of Documents. The sheer volume of the work handled in this office makes it impossible for all errors to be caught and corrected before the *Monthly Catalog* is printed and the shipping lists are duplicated for distribution. Therefore, a system for handling mistakes in the *Monthly Catalog* has been developed; corrections for previous catalogs are listed in the front of each issue of the *Monthly Catalog*. Shipping lists also are corrected periodically by a correction sheet, which lists the errors discovered in previous lists.

The procedures described below have been developed to insure that a periodic and systematic approach will be used in handling all corrections. If these corrections are not made, then the *Monthly Catalog* and library records will not match the records of the Superintendent of Documents and other depositories.

This would destroy the advantages of using the Superintendent of Documents classification system and interlibrary cooperation within the depository system.

Monthly Catalog Corrections

Corrections appear in the front of the *Monthly Catalog* (Figure 7.1). Find the issue designated in the correction and make the change in entry as specified (Figure 7.2). These changes will be permanent, so all marks should be legible. Check off each correction as it is made, and initial each list.

Check the shelf list to assure that it agrees with the new number and make any needed changes on the shelf list cards, material on the shelves, and other records.

Figure 7.1

DECEMBER 1972

Corrections for Previous Monthly Catalogs

Feb. 1972. Entry 2005. Federal reclamation projects, water & land resource accomplishments, 1970. [1971.] vii+50 p. il. 4° † ● Item 663–A I 27.55 : 970 Insert this entry in proper sequence.

May 1972. Entry 6921, Correct heading to read: Consumer information series. (Federal Supply Service.) ● Item 558–A–2 GS 2.16 : (nos.).

June 1972. Entry 8758, Report of 2d international technical conference on experimental safety vehicles . . . Oct. 26–29, 1971. Correct class to read TD 8.16 : 971–2.

July 1972. Entry 9812, Correct heading to read: Consumer information series. (Federal Supply Service.) ● Item 558–A–2 GS 2.16 : (nos.).

Aug. 1972. Entry 11348, National Clearinghouse for Mental Health Information. Correct class to read HE 20.2402 : N 21/3.

Oct. 1972. Entry 12743, Department of Interior and related agencies appropriations for fiscal year 1973. Correct L.C. card number to read 72–602208.

Shipping List Corrections

Complete depositories will make all corrections. Selective depositories should check the item numbers with the "Items Selected List" (discussed in Chapter 5) to be sure that the library received that publication. (If the item is not one selected, put an "X" by the number.) For those items the library does receive, pull the shipping lists that need correcting and find the item on the list that was incorrectly identified. Pull the shelf list card for the incorrect number and correct the card as necessary. (Erase if the item does not belong there, etc.) Make a new shelf list card, if needed, or add the corrected information to the proper shelf list card. Make the necessary correction on the publication itself. Check off each correction on the list as it is made. Place the correction list with the shipping list that it accompanied. Make the correction on the necessary shipping list and refile. *Be sure that all the corrections are made on all necessary cards, publications, and lists.* (See Appendix C for sample shipping list corrections).

Figure 7.2

GOVERNMENT PUBLICATIONS

**NATIONAL INSTITUTE OF ALLERGY AND INFECTIOUS
DISEASES, Health, Education, and Welfare Dept.
Bethesda, MD   20014**

11346 Manual of tissue typing techniques [with lists of references]; edited by
John G. Ray, jr. [and others]. Apr. 1972. [5]+86 p. il. 4°   (Transplanta-
tion and Immunology Branch, Collaborative Research.)   †   ● Item
505–A–2   HE 20.3258 : T 52

**NATIONAL INSTITUTE OF MENTAL HEALTH, Health, Education,
and Welfare Dept., Chevy Chase, MD   20015**

11347 Mental health research grant awards, fiscal year 1971; prepared by Pro-
gram Analysis and Evaluation Section, Division of Extramural Research
Programs. [1972.] viii+67 p. ([DHEW publication (HSM) 72–9078].)
* Paper, 40c.   ● Item 507–B–11   HE 20.2423 : 971

11348 National Clearinghouse for Mental Health Information, serving the professional community and concerned public. [1972.] [2]+12+[2] p. il.
oblong 24° ([DHEW publication (HSM) 72–9047.])   * Paper, 20c.
(S/N 1724–0217).   ● Item 507–B–5   HE 20.2402 :
N 21/3

In this example, the error was for a depository item and the entry
was probably correct on the shipping list. Check the shelf to verify
and correct any records that were incorrect.

SEARCHING FOR ENTRIES AND
CLASSIFICATION NUMBERS

If the Superintendent of Documents classification is to be effective, each
library must undertake to use the same identification number and entry for every
item. Verifying classification numbers is sometimes easy, but very frequently it
involves a frustrating search through a number of sources. Many agencies do not
send a copy of every publication to the Public Documents Department Library, so
there are times when even an exhaustive search ends in failure.

Official sources—*Monthly Catalog*, item card, *List of Classes*, shelf list—do not
always agree exactly on the form of entry for the agency, or even, sometimes, on
the agency itself. When discrepancies occur, the librarian must choose the form he
will use. The *List of Classes* should be the very last source used for verification,
since it apparently does not attempt to be precise. The item card might seem to
be final authority, but it is the *Monthly Catalog* entry upon which patrons base
their request. The shelf list gives the entry used in the particular documents library.
Each source has its advantages, and circumstances may alter cases.

Basic steps are as follows: Examine the publication to determine the subject,
issuing agency, personal author (if any), and date of copyright or publication.
Search the appropriate tool. *It is sometimes difficult to decide whether to search
the entry first, or the class number.*

Many tools published by various government agencies will help supply correct bibliographic information for the material at hand, if the piece itself is insufficient. It is sometimes necessary to approach Poore, or Ames, or the *Document Catalog*, or the *Monthly Catalog* or some other index to verify the source of the document in question.

Having then determined—from a source other than the document itself, if necessary—the exact description, it now remains to assign its proper Superintendent of Documents classification.

Chapter 3 discusses some of the major tools presently available. There are others that could have been cited, and announcements concerning new bibliographies and indexes appear with increasing frequency. Those mentioned cover a broad spectrum of types and agencies, most of them being all-inclusive for the period covered. Many of the newer offerings concentrate on an area or an agency. Those mentioned in this chapter are especially useful for verification of entries and/ or classification numbers.

The tools have been divided into two parts. Search for serials will lead to one set of books; monographs will be found through others. Suggestions are made for classifying material that cannot be found in any of these sources but that would normally fall within the range of interest of the government documents sphere.

Tools for Serials

Tools for serials include the following:

1. John L. Andriot, *Guide to U.S. Government Serials and Periodicals.*
2. *Checklist of United States Public Documents 1789-1909.*
3. *Checklist of United States Public Documents, 1789-1970.* A dual media edition of the U.S. Superintendent of Documents Public Documents Library Shelflist, with accompanying indexes. It has a semi-annual updating service for shelflist and indexes.
4. Daniel Lester and Marilyn A. Lester. *United States Government Serial Publications 1789-1972. A Preliminary Edition.* October 1972.
5. *List of Classes of United States Government Publications Available for Selection by Depository Libraries.*
6. *Monthly Catalog of U.S. Government Publications.*
7. Mary Elizabeth Poole, *Documents Office Classification.* 1966.
8. Main entry and series title files maintained by the library are arranged alphabetically and will provide the class stem number, main entry, and title for any series held by the library.

Tools for Monographs

Tools for monographs include the *Checklist*, an agency index allows this approach, and the histories of the agencies give another method of search. Earlier-later class numbers trace series. Poole's *Documents Office Classification for Cuttered Publications 1910-1924*; the *Monthly Catalog*; the *Shelflist of the*

Superintendent of Documents, which allows for either direct search by class number or indirect search through book indexes; and Przebienda's cumulative personal author index to the *Monthly Catalog*.

Once the correct classification is established (*be sure that the bibliographic description in the catalog completely matches the one in the publication*) follow basic checking procedure. If the publication cannot be identified, note in pencil in the upper right-hand corner the first and last dates searched (e.g., 70-72/6). Place the publication with other unidentified material for later searches. If all sources have been consulted and classification numbers have still not been found, it will be necessary to assign the classification.

Steps in Assigning Classification Numbers for Publications Never Listed

1. Check the issuing department, and determine from this the class letters such as A, C, D, Y 3, etc.

2. Check subordinate bureau for number following letter (such as A 1. for Secretary of Agriculture, C 13. for National Bureau of Standards, D 301. for Air Force).

3. Check for any series number. Use this series as a class if there is a series. Otherwise, ask yourself these questions:

    a. Is it a periodical or otherwise recurring publication that has a separate class? The preface may say it is the first of a series of annual (quarterly, monthly, etc.) publications for which a new class should be established. It may be the annual report of a department.

    b. Is it a bibliography?

    c. Is it an address or lecture given before a group?

    d. Is it a handbook, manual, or guide (which usually can be determined from title, preface, or foreword)?

    e. Is it regulations, rules, or instructions (which usually can be determined from title, preface, or foreword)?

    f. Is it a law or an act, and does it therefore belong in a "laws" class?

4. If the publication does not fit into any of these categories, it is usually a "General publication."

5. For monographs, find the class stem number which most closely fits the publication. From a two-figure Cutter table, determine the Cutter number for the piece. (An optional procedure is to use the three figure Cutter table, as the Library at the Superintendent of Documents does for materials acquired but not published by a government agency.) Add a raised zero (^{0}) to the Cutter number to indicate that this number is assumed. In the appropriate index, give subject and call number.

6. For serials, find the class stem number that most closely fits the publication. Assign a series number that would be higher than any anticipated by the agency. Type cards and indicate the date the series was cataloged.

Steps 1 through 4 of this procedure were described on a form entitled *Steps in Assigning Classification Numbers and Item Numbers.* This form was sent out by the Superintendent of Documents in March 1973.

CHANGES MADE BY THE
SUPERINTENDENT OF DOCUMENTS

Over the years, the functions and activities of the federal government have expanded so greatly that periodic reorganizations of the federal departments and agencies have become necessary. These reorganizations affect certain bibliographic data pertaining to the publications issued by the agencies involved. The movement of an agency from one department to another will necessitate, at the least, a change in the classification number of the agency's publications, which in turn necessitates changes in the main entry cards, title cards, item number cards, and shelf list cards.

In cases where a series has changed its classification number more than once, the librarian will have to make a decision concerning the location of the materials. If strict adherence to the Superintendent of Documents system is desired, then cross references on the cards and shelves must be made. If, however, the librarian decides—all disadvantages aside—that it would be better to arrange the publications all under one number, then the number on the old publications must be changed and cross references reflecting what has happened must be made on the shelf list cards and shelves. There is no clear-cut, hard-and-fast rule for making this decision; the decision must be based on the individual situation.

Other changes made by the Superintendent of Documents may include the addition of new series title to an item number card, the discontinuance of a series, or a change in author and/or title. All of these eventualities require changes in, and/or new records for, the publications.

One of the special problems in the area of changes made by the Superintendent of Documents is catching the changes. Sometimes these are overlooked or missed for a variety of reasons; once the item has slipped through unnoticed, it is difficult to trace the mistake or oversight.

Changes in classification and cataloging may result from the reorganization or the renaming of the corporate body. And this newly established entity almost inevitably brings about changes in titles of old series, or the merging of an established series into a new one. These changes do not necessarily occur at one time. Therefore, to have complete control over the entire file, it will be essential to give holdings that are exactly coordinated with agencies.

Some of the changes are easy to follow and require only one set of references. Others are complicated, and to follow all their convolutions is a tedious and sometimes seemingly impossible task.

The examples below will show how the changes are discovered, and how the records will reflect the evolution.

The Cataloging Section of the Library of the Superintendent of Documents Office prepares the *Daily Depository Shipping List* that accompanies each shipment of materials to the depository libraries.

The Library there is not a reference collection, so there is no constant pressure to retrieve a specific document in a hurry, or to identify the many stages of change in agencies or output. The shipping lists formerly did not elaborate upon the changed status of material shipped. With encouragement from librarians working in the field, the catalogers began to add more information; since early 1973, they have given almost all information needed to establish a one-step change.

The same situation obtained in the listing of new series, when the note said only "This new series is being added to this item number." The wording on the shipping list has now been changed to indicate a reason for the alteration, as indicated below:

231–A   Note: Change in class from C42.2 to C57.102 due to change in issuing agency (International Commerce Bureau, General publications)

or

315-D   Tech memo. . .   D5.110
         Note: This new class added to this Item number (Technicians memorandum series)

The steps illustrated below are applicable at any level of information available. Some of them presuppose a depository item that is not fully identified on a shipping list, and follow each stage of identification. Permanent information is typed, and any part not positively cataloged by SuDocs is left blank. When the missing information is verified in a recognized tool (*Monthly Catalog*, shelf list, *Checklist*, etc.), this information is added and all records are then completed.

Provision is made to incorporate into the collection material that is not listed in the catalogs with the documents number, but that is within the provenance of the collection. The suggestions conform to the guidelines of the SuDocs library as they catalog pieces that come to them.

There is presently no one place where the whole history of a series or an organization may be found. The *Checklist* gives earlier and later information at each point. The *Monthly Catalog* gives the immediately preceding class number. Thus, the name of the agency and other identities needs must be searched elsewhere. Poole gives earlier and later numbers, but not the names of agencies and holdings at each stage. The indexes of the dual media edition of the *Checklist . . . 1789-1970* and its supplements again fail to give complete information. At last notice, the SuDocs library does not have the entire history of a series all in one place. The working librarian must ferret out all relevant materials and must write for himself the story of the agency, its work, and its publications.

The "New Classification Numbers Added" section of the *Monthly Catalog* does not indicate other changes that may have occurred to a series. For example, title change is not indicated here, and official recognition of the continuation must be sought elsewhere. Serials, or periodical type material are usually identified now in the February Supplement of the *Monthly Catalog.* Titles are arranged in alphabetical order. More often than not, the earlier title is given, together with the last volume and number of the old classification. But many times it is here impossible to tell just what level of the hierarchy of a complicated bureau has been taken as the issuing agency. This information frequently can only be inferred from the general number of the assigned class. A search of the shelf list also fails to reveal the information, since the entry is frequently omitted on the card. When the series is a numbered one, the *Monthly Catalog* does not indicate the last number in the old series.

It is relatively easy to keep records on a volume-number series, or on one whose parts are indicated only by date. But numbered series present difficulties. If an old numbered publication is revised, it is likely that the original was under the old title, or old classification number, and the revised version under the new. The problem then arises as to how to indicate on the shelf list that the old one has been revised. And, if earlier editions of publications are ordinarily discarded, it is equally difficult to decide whether old editions in different numbers are to be weeded or kept, and whether old records should be closed out.

Again, if the name of the agency changes and the classification number stays the same, the new name of the agency and the old class number do not appear in the New Classification Numbers section. These changes are caught initially only if every publication is carefully examined, and if the title and agency on the piece in hand are compared to the shelf list card. Later, however, these changes may be found in an examination of the *Monthly Catalog* or other tools, and the discrepancy will be noted at that time.

Title Changes

When a series title is changed, pull the item number card and make a new card for the changed title, typing in only those parts that are verified. Clip this to the old item card and file.

Figure 7.3—New Item Card

```
Item No.  88-C




                                                    A77.710

          SL  3010;  10.3.63
```

Make a new check card (Figure 7.4). Put only the information that has been verified, and put the old title at bottom of card. Be sure to put the item number on the back of the check card.

Figure 7.4

Yr.	Vol.	Ja.	F	Mr.	Ap.	My.	Je.	Jl.	Ag.	S	O	N	D	T. P. and I.
1963										✓	✓		✓	

A77.710 U.S.   *3*

Earlier title Nutrition . Committee news

Library Form No. 24

Pull old check card. Type at bottom "Title changed to _____" (Figure 7.5). Then, search for the entry in the *Monthly Catalog* (February Supplement) and for the first entry under the new name. Complete all cards. (Figure 7.6 illustrates a completed item number card and Figure 7.7 illustrates a completed shelf list card.)

Figure 7.5

A77.710   U.S. Agricultural Research Service.
Nutrition Committee news

Yr.	Vol.	Ja.	F	Mr.	Ap.	My.	Je.	Jl.	Ag.	S	O	N	D	T. P. and I.
1961						✓			✓		✓		✓	
1962			✓		✓		✓		✓		✓		✓	
1963			✓		✓		✓		✓					

Title changed to Nutrition program news
with Sept. 1963.

Library Form No. 24

Figure 7.6

Item No. 88-C

AGRICULTURAL RESEARCH SERVICE

Nutrition Program News   A77.710

SL 3010; 10.3.63

Feb. 1964 M.C.

Figure 7.7

A77.710 U.S. Agricultural Research Service. Nutrition program news													
Yr.	Vol.	Ja.	F	Mr.	Ap.	My.	Je.	Jl.	Ag.	S	O	N	D	T. P. and I.
1963										✓	✓		✓	
1964			✓		✓		✓		✓		✓		✓	
1965			✓		✓		✓		✓		✓		✓	
1966			✓		✓		✓		✓		✓		✓	
1967			✓		✓		✓		✓		✓		✓	
1968			✓		✓		✓		✓		✓		✓	
1969			✓		✓		✓		✓		✓		✓	
1970			✓		✓		✓		✓		✓		✓	
1971			✓		✓		✓		✓		✓		✓	

Earlier title: Nutrition Committee news
Library Form No. 24

Make new author and title cards (Figures 7.8 and 7.9) with cross references to the old title. Add cross references to old cards.

Figure 7.8

```
A77.710   U.S. Agricultural Research Service
             Nutrition program news.


             Before Sep.-Oct. 1963, see

A77.710   U.S. Agricultural Research Service.
             Nutrition Committee news.
```

Figure 7.9

```
A77.710         Nutrition Committee news.
         U.S. Agricultural Research Service.

             Beginning Sep.-Oct. 1963,

             title changed to

A77.710  U.S. Agricultural Research Service.
             Nutrition program news.
```

Classification Number Changes

When the organizational structure of the government changes, classification changes also occur. First, follow the procedures given for a change in series title, changing the classification number instead of the title. Then search the *Monthly Catalog* (New Classifications Added, February Supplement, and for the first entry under the new number). Complete all cards.

The illustrations so far have been relatively simple and uncomplicated. It is true that the new title and new number had to be searched and verified in catalogs that appeared long after the changes took place, but the explanations found were clear and precise.

Before we proceed to more complex changes, it seems fit to illustrate some problems that arise and that are not soon settled by the SuDocs Library—and indeed, that are perhaps never noted there. But the individual institution must cope with the situation immediately. The examples given are for depository series, but similar situations could arise with non-depository material.

Discrepancies Between Sources

The first situation is one in which the Shipping List gives one issuing agency and the *Monthly Catalog* gives another. This same problem can arise when the original item is identified with its own item card. As indicated earlier, the individual library must decide which authority to follow; cross references can lead to the other suggested entry, so that the searcher can locate the needed material.

In this situation the original item card showed the Census Bureau as author. However, shipping list 6833;3.30.73 listed the Social and Economic Statistics Administration as the issuing agency for the new classification number. A check of other numbers close to this, including C56.213, indicated that the Census Bureau had continued to be called the responsible agency. Thus, a new item card was made, but the issuing agency was left blank. When the July 1973 *Monthly Catalog* was received, it showed the issuing agency to be the Census Bureau. The new item card was completed and a note was made to show what had happened. All other cards were then completed giving the Census Bureau as issuing body and making the same note. Another author card was then made under U.S. Social and Economic Statistics Administration, with a *see* reference to Census Bureau.

Same Classification Number Used on Different Items

The other example is one in which the same classification number was assigned to what would appear to be two different series (see Figures 7.10 and 7.11). At least two names were given as series identification, and some of the publications were numbered and some were cuttered. Cross references at all points are necessary for access to the material.

Apparently an assignment was made to the original papers, which were non-depository; when the depository status of a group of papers concerning day care was established, the difference was not discovered.

Steps needed to clarify the identification of the papers on day care are illustrated below. Notes on the original item card should be added by the individual library and the library should also make an additional item card to show the relation between the series. This second item card seems to be needed because the cuttered publications are not depository and the double entry is therefore clarified. The material was originally checked with no difficulty; it was only later that all the other cards were made, and the cross references and notes added.

Figure 7.10—Original Item Card with Note Added

```
Item No. 454-C-3

   CHILD DEVELOPMENT OFFICE, Health,
      Education and Welfare Dept.

Day Care USA (publications)              HE21.11:
   Some publications are Cuttered, with no obvious
series identification. (They are not Depository)
(MC1971 New clss)
Child Development: Day Care              HE21.11:nos.
   carries an obvious series designation and is
   listed in the Monthly Catalog entries under this
   same number and Item.          (8.4.73)
12.11.70
```

Figure 7.11—Second Item Number Card with Note Added

```
Item No. 454-C-3

   CHILD DEVELOPMENT OFFICE, Health,
      Education and Welfare Dept.

Child Development: Day Care              HE21.11:nos.
   carries an obvious series identification and is
   listed in the Monthly Catalog entries under this
   number and Item.

Day Care USA (publications)              HE21.11:
   is given on original Item card and is entry in
   Monthly Catalog New Classification Numbers. These
   carry no obvious series identification, are
   cuttered, and are not Depository items.
   (8.4.73)
```

The same basic procedures should be followed on shelf list, author, and title cards. Cross references from one to the other help clarify the situation.

Multiple Changes

The following examples (Figures 7.12a through 7.12e) show how a number of problems develop. A single title was selected to represent three situations. It is not often that such a series will be found, but the trouble can arise in different combinations or singly.

Figure 7.12a–Original Item Card

```
Item No. 42-J



            ECONOMIC RESEARCH SERVICE

Foreign Gold & Dollar Reserves                    A93.34
   Current Trends



   1.9.70
```

Figure 7.12b–Item Card for New Series

```
Item No. 42-J


        ECONOMIC RESEARCH SERVICE
World Monetary Conditions in Relation          A93.34/2
       to Agricultural Needs

           SL 6241; 12.28.71

NOT VERIFIED IN MONTHLY CATALOG THROUGH OCT. 1973.
```

Figure 7.12c–Shelf List Card for Monograph
(original publication with
added notes)

A93.2 U.S. Economic Research Service.
        General publications.

G57   Foreign gold and dollar reserves. 1962.
        For later issues, see A93.34; A93.34/2

Figure 7.12d–Check Card for Original Series with Added Notes

A93.34 U.S. Economic Research Service.
        Foreign gold and dollar reserves.

1951	1961	✔1971	1981	1991	2001	2011	2021
1952	1962	1972	1982	1992	2002	2012	2022
1953	✔1963	1973	1983	1993	2003	2013	2023
1954	1964	1974	1984	1994	2004	2014	2024
1955	1965	1975	1985	1995	2005	2015	2025
1956	1966	1976	1986	1996	2006	2016	2026
1957	1967	1977	1987	1997	2007	2017	2027
1958	1968	1978	1988	1998	2008	2018	2028
1959	*✔1969	1979	1989	1999	2009	2019	2029
1960	✔1970	1980	1990	2000	2010	2020	2030

*1st dep. copy
                Earlier A93.2; G57 Later A93.34/2

Figure 7.12e–Check Card for Later Series

A93.34[2]	U.S. Economic Research Service. World monetary conditions in relation to agricultural needs.							
1951	1961	⌐1971 ┐	1981	1991	2001	2011	2021
1952	1962	⌐1972 ₂	1982	1992	2002	2012	2022
1953	1963	✓1973 ✝	1983	1993	2003	2013	2023
1954	1964	1974	1984	1994	2004	2014	2024
1955	1965	1975	1985	1995	2005	2015	2025
1956	1966	1976	1986	1996	2006	2016	2026
1957	1967	1977	1987	1997	2007	2017	2027
1958	1968	1978	1988	1998	2008	2018	2028
1959	1969	1979	1989	1999	2009	2019	2029
1960	1970	1980	1990	2000	2010	2020	2030

Earlier A93.2:G57: A93.34

The original item card gave no hint of an earlier history. The new number has never been listed in the "New Classifications Added," so the only verification of the fact that it does in fact supersede another is the note on the shipping list.

This series, then, can be traced partly through the *Monthly Catalog*, partly through the shipping lists, but not all stages can be verified in the proper manner. Since this series has not been listed in a period of over two years, it seems sensible to add the name of the agency and the name of the series to the check cards, and to make all author and title cards with the proper cross references. The item card retains the note that the second series has not been listed.

In other words, at some time the librarian on the scene must step in and make an independent judgment as to when to do original cataloging, and when to assume that official entry will not be forthcoming and to proceed with completion of records as seems best.

Previous illustrations have provided step-by-step directions for the procedures of making author and title cards for the original number of a series, and for indicating a change in status in a single instance, whether it be author, title, or classification. This can be expanded for many changes, and the complete history of changes will be seen on the card at a glance.

The examples that follow are multi-stage development, in which there are changes in classification, agency, and then again in classification, in successive moves. Each of the changes is recorded as it takes place; all these are put here to illustrate the entire process. If other reorganization is effected, or a new title replaces the old, the procedure outlined here will be continued to reflect the new situation.

First, pull the item number card. Make a new card for new situations, typing only verified information. File at front of old cards, which would be in order chronologically. Pull all cards (i.e., shelf list, author, and title). Make all references on each card so that the series may be traced from any source. Make dummies for each number the publication has had, with all cross references. Refile all cards.

Sometimes changes are multiple, as in the case of *Hydraulic Engineering Circulars*, which changed classification number, then agency, then classification number again. It was first published by the Public Roads Bureau under C37.4/2. The classification was later changed to TD 2.104. Still later, the issuing agency changed to Federal Highway Administration and the classification became TD 2.27. These changes are reflected in the library's files when one follows the steps given under "Changes in Identification" earlier in this chapter. It should be noted that only one title card is retained. The changes should be recorded on it for quick reference to earlier issues.

Agency Change Cards

A device not previously mentioned may prove useful when an agency develops through a number of changes—of name, of absorption, or of classification. At the beginning of the listings for each such agency, both shelf and agency/series lists, file a colored, tabbed card, with the agency's entire history, in chronological order (see Figure 7.13).

Figure 7.13

```
          Road Inquiry Office.
             1894-1916/July 11
          Public Roads Office and Rural Engineering Office
             July 11/1916-1918/July
  A22.    Public Roads Bureau (Agriculture)
             July/1918-1939/June 30
  FW2.    Public Roads Administration (FWA)
             July 1/1939-1949/June 30
  GS3.    Public Roads Bureau (GSA)
             June 30/1949-1949/Aug. 20
  C37.    Public Roads Bureau (Commerce)
             Aug. 20/1949-1966/Oct. 15
  TD2.    Federal Highway Administration (Transportation
             Oct. 15/1966--                     Dept.)
```

Making Dummies and Relocating Publications

Each time a publication changes classification number, it is necessary to make provisions for locating it on the shelves. The usual method is to prepare dummies with pertinent information, and to put them where the book would stand. For each number the publication has had, there should be a dummy on the shelf. All dummies should contain all cross references, so that the patron will find the complete series, no matter what its changed situation. It seems best to have on the spine only the call number being identified. The other numbers will be on the face of the dummy. Most people like to have the title of the series on the spine, because this is what browsers frequently look for.

Type a card for face of the dummy. No matter how many changes of identification a series may have, continue to make dummies for each situation. Perhaps the easiest way for any change after the first is simply to make sufficient copies of the basic history card to afford one for each agency and each title and for one dummy on the shelf at each point. Thus, each place will give agency, title, and inclusive holdings at every point. The same history card will go on the face of every dummy. A label with title and call number will be necessary, but typing these will be a minor chore.

The card used here as an example (Figure 7.14) was one made with the title repeated at every instance. If the title remains the same, it need not appear on the history card until the heading is typed for each entry. Again, if the name of the agency stays the same at all or some places, it need not appear after the first mention. This will save space on the card for any future changes, as well as time and effort in typing.

Figure 7.14

```
  A29.6  U.S. Weather Bureau.
            Monthly weather review.
            v.15-68; 1887-1939
  C30.14 U.S. Weather Bureau.
            Monthly weather review.
            v.68-98; 1940-1970.
  C55.11 U.S. National Oceanic and Atmospheric
            Administration.
            Monthly weather review.
            v.99-       ; 1971-
```

When moving earlier issues of a publication to a new location because of a new classification number, mark all cards "Shelved under _____ ."

Preceding examples have shown how to trace the history of publications through changes of title, changes of classification due to reorganization of a higher department, and changes of classification due to change of issuing agency.

Publications sometimes cease completely. Note to this effect must be made on all cards. Source of verification is essential. If unverified, this should also be indicated.

The *VISTA Fact Book* is a good illustration of a number of points. It has changed issuing agency and thus classification. This change was verified in the *Monthly Catalog*. It later ceased publication. This was not known immediately at the Library of the Superintendent of Documents, for there was a note that they would supply later issues if available. Later, it was superseded by a new publication of expanded coverage. The introduction of the new publication gave this information; a year and a half later, the *Monthly Catalog* has not listed the latest classification number in the "New Classifications Added" section, and the entry in the February Supplement makes no note of an earlier history.

The cards that follow (Figures 7.15a through 7.15c) are self-explanatory. They follow principles previously discussed and illustrated.

When items are discontinued by the Superintendent of Documents, pull the item card. Type "Discontinued as Depository Item with (number, date, etc.)," date, and then verify the source of information (see Figures 7.16a through 7.16c).

Figure 7.15a—Original Item Number Card

```
Item No. 857-H-13

ECONOMIC OPPORTUNITY OFFICE, Executive Office of
        the President

VISTA Fact Book               PrEx10.21

   Consists largely of a directory of current projects,
but also includes current statistics concerning
VISTA Volunteers as well as information on the growth
of VISTA.

   10.13.677
```

Figure 7.15b–First Change. Verified. Discontinued.
Unverified except in succeeding
publication.

Item No. 857-H-13

ACTION

VISTA Fact Book   AA1.9

    SL 6152; 10.14.71

       Discontinued with May 1972 issue.
       See June 1972 AA1.9/2

    Feb. 1972 MC

Figure 7.15c–Second Change. Classification Unverified.
History unverified except in Introduction.

Item No. 857-H-13

ACTION

Domestic Programs Fact Book   AA1.9/2

    SL 6548; 8.8.72

    Supersedes AA1.9. See introduction, June 1972

not verified through Oct. 1973 MC

Figure 7.16a

```
Item No. 544-A


    GENERAL ACCOUNTING OFFICE

GAO Review                          GA1.15

    This Item no. is being cancelled.
    Future issues will not be available to
depository libraries.

      SL 3926: 3.28.66
3.11.66
```

Figure 7.16b

```
Item No. 544-A (Rev.)

    GENERAL ACCOUNTING OFFICE

GAO Review (quarterly)             GA1.15

    Published as a source of information and ideas to
encourage professional development in the accounting
and auditing staffs of the General Accounting Office.



    11.21.66
```

Figure 7.16c

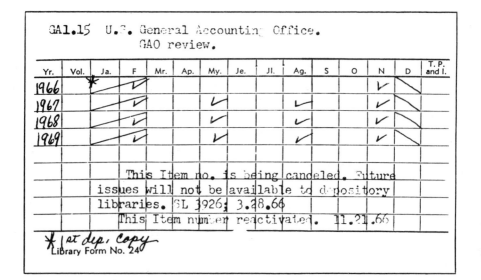

GA1.15 U.S. General Accounting Office.
GAO review.

Yr.	Vol.	Ja.	F	Mr.	Ap.	My.	Je.	Jl.	Ag.	S	O	N	D	T. P. and I.
1966			✓									✓		
1967			✓			✓			✓			✓		
1968			✓			✓			✓			✓		
1969			✓			✓			✓			✓		

This Item no. is being canceled. Future
issues will not be available to depository
libraries. SL 3926; 3.28.66
This Item number reactivated. 11.21.66

Library Form No. 24

Chapter 8

ADDITIONAL PROCESSES

The preceding chapters have presented the main and specialized technical processing procedures that must take place in some form in a depository library, especially those libraries that maintain a separate collection. These procedures, however, are not the only tasks that must be dealt with by documents librarians.

The purpose of this chapter is to provide selected guidelines for managing some of the everyday problems or tasks. It would be impossible to mention every situation which might arise. Some of the major ones that will be defined by this chapter are: 1) highlighting sub-series which are not fully identified by Superintendent of Documents cataloging; 2) selective cataloging for partially integrated collections; 3) transferring or reclassifying documents; 4) weeding; 5) binding; and 6) circulation principles.

HIGHLIGHTING SUB-SERIES

In several instances, the Superintendent of Documents classification scheme has established one main entry and series title for a group of publications. It has then placed a number of publications in various sub-groupings or sub-series within that main entry and classification. This can be frustrating for both the librarian and the user, since a particular sub-series classed this way cannot be identified without a long searching process, which is a waste of valuable time. Prime examples of lost sub-series are the *Biographic Registers* of the State Department, *Library Statistics of Colleges and Universities*, monographs that later became serials but were not assigned a unique serial number, and the Committees and Commissions of the President.

In processing, one can simply leave the material buried in the sub-series grouping as the Superintendent of Documents scheme provides, or one can highlight the series by creating special author, title, and shelf list cards that reflect the sub-series entry in a prominent place. Sometimes the issuing agency never separates an on-going sub-series from the original series, which makes identification difficult. The following example illustrates this: the *Biographic Register* is a part of a larger series. Each issue was numbered in the regular series sequence from 1948 until the

1966 edition; at that time the number 126 was reserved for the title, and the date became a necessary part of the call number.

The first issue was checked on a standard 1-100 card (see Figure 8.1a) with no note to distinguish it. When the second edition was received as a part of the series but with a different number, a note as to the title of the first and second issue was made. With the appearance of the third in the series, a separate card was set up (Figure 8.1b), and a note added to the series check indicated that the user should see the following card. At this point, too, a separate author and title card was made and filed for the convenience of the public (Figures 8.1c and 8.1d).

Another kind of "lost" series is a series that first appeared as a monograph and was later expanded into a series.

The U.S. Department of Agriculture sponsored an Honor Awards Ceremony in 1949, and published the proceedings of the day. Apparently the idea of the awards was appealing, and the Department made awards in later years, and published the activities. This began as a monograph and was assigned a Cutter number as its book number. The proceedings of later years were assigned the same book number, and the date of the ceremony covered became a part of the identification of the book.

The check card used may be of two kinds: the original card may be used, with each new publication added, or an annual card may be substituted. The former can show more clearly, perhaps, the month and day of the ceremony. If not all publications were received, some space should be left on the first card for the added entries that might be acquired later. When it was determined that the Department would continue to publish this, the new cards for author and title were made.

Since this serial is not a part of a series with its own distinctive title, it is not necessary to indicate the generalized category on the author or title cards. This could also be omitted on the annual check cards. It should appear on a plain check card, so that the filer will have no difficulty in finding its proper place in the shelf list.

Chapter 7 of this manual concerns itself with complete identification of series and agencies that change names or identification. It describes at some length ways in which the complete history of an organization or series may be traced. While this is all valid procedure, there are times when a title changes so slightly that it may not be necessary to list each and every variation. In this case, it is sufficient to add the note "Title varies," and to indicate that not all the titles are separately identified.

Committees and Commissions of Congress and the President do not follow the established patterns for entries on the author, title, and check cards. This is due in part to the variations in the meaning of the classification number. Whereas the series title in a standard number is designated between the period and the colon, Congressional and Presidential Committee series are designated either by a number or cuttered number following the colon—i.e., Pr37.8:*P93*/ or Y3.Or3:*2*/. In this case, then, to have meaningful author and title cards one must move beyond the general series title (Committees and Commissions of the President or Congress) and tell which committee and/or what series of publications the committee is issuing—i.e., U.S. President of the United States, Committees and Commissions of the President—President's Task Force on Prisoner Rehabilitation. In this entry, the only real title with meaning for the public is the name of the organization.

Figure 8.1a–Original Check Card

S1.69 U.S. State Department.
        Department and Foreign Service series.

1948

1	⊢11	21	⌐31	41	⌐51	⌐61	⌐71	⌐81	⌐91
2	12	⌐22	⌐32⊬	⌐42	⌐52⊬	⌐62	⌐72	82	⌐92⊬
✓3	13	⌐23	⌐33⌐	⌐43	✓53	⌐63	⌐73	83	⌐93⌐
✓4	⊢14	⌐24⌐	⌐34	⌐44	✓54	⌐64	⌐74	⌐84	94
⌐5	15	⌐25⌐	⌐35⊬	⌐45	⌐55⌐	⌐65⊬	⌐75⊬	85	⌐95
⌐6	⌐16	⌐26	⌐36	⌐46⌐	⌐56	⌐66	⌐76	⌐86⊬	⌐96
⌐7	⌐17	⌐27	⌐37⌐	⌐47	⌐57	⌐67	⌐77⌐	87	⌐97
⌐8	⌐18	⌐28	38⌐	⌐48	·58	⌐68⌐	⌐78	⌐88	⌐98
⌐9	⌐19	⌐29	39⌐	⌐49	·59	⌐69	⌐79	⌐89⌐	·99
10	⌐20	⌐30	40⌐	⌐50	60	✓70	80	90	⏐00⊬

* Biographic register see following cards # Foreign consular offic

Figure 8.1b–New Card for Series

S1.69 U.S. State Department.
        Department and Foreign Service.
                The biographic register

1951 no.24	1961	⌐1971 126	1981	1991	2001	2011	2021
⌐1952 26	1962	⌐1972 126	1982	1992	2002	2012	2022
⌐1953	⌐1963	⌐1973 126	1983	1993	2003	2013	2023
⌐1954	⌐1964	1974	1984	1994	2004	2014	2024
⌐1955 96	1965 ¢	1975	1985	1995	2005	2015	2025
⌐1956	⌐1966 126	1976	1986	1996	2006	2016	2026
⌐1957	⌐1967 126	1977	1987	1997	2007	2017	2027
⌐1958	⌐1968	1978	1988	1998	2008	2018	2028
⌐1959	⌐1969	1979	1989	1999	2009	2019	2029
⌐1960	⌐1970	1980	1990	2000	2010	2020	2030

Library Form No. 21B

Figure 8.1c–Author Card

```
S1.69  U.S. State Department.
              Biographic register.

              subseries of

       Department and Foreign Service series.
```

Figure 8.1d–Title Card

```
S1.69         Biographic register.
         U.S. State Department.

              Subseries of
       Department and Foreign Service series.
```

In working with committees of the President, one must remember that the entries on the item number cards are *not used.* This is the only case where this is true. However, when a new Congressional committee is established or a new series by a Congressional committee is started, new item number cards must be typed with the name of the Congressional committee as the main entry and the series title, the title of the series for that particular committee. In the case of item no. 1089– Commissions, Committees and Boards, Reports and Publications Y3.–this means that each time a new commission is appointed, a new item number card will be added to the file and the series will be treated exactly as we treat new classes added to any item number. *Remember that no author, title, or shelf list card should have an author entry like commissions, committees, and boards or a title entry like reports and publications.*

An example of the procedure for presidential committees follows.

Figure 8.2—Established Item Card

```
Item No. 851-J

      PRESIDENT OF UNITED STATES

Committees and Commissions of the President   Pr34.8
   Note.--This item number will cover those special
Committees and commissions appointed by the President
to perform specific studies and whose existence ceases
after reports are made. Standing committees or com-
missions for which item numbers have already been es-
tablished will not come under this distribution. [For
any numbers added to this card, use the name of the
Committee for the Main entry.
This Item number will be used for later Presidents
also]   (UK Note)
```

In Figure 8.2, the note in brackets is added by the individual library.

Routines described above for establishing new entries will not obtain in this case. The new numbers section of the *Monthly Catalog* does not list the Presidential Committees. The publications of the committees are given, with full bibliographical description, in the main body of the *Monthly Catalog* under the heading of the President.

Therefore, when a publication is received from a committee not previously listed, make a new item card. Type on it the item number, committee name, name of series, shipping list number and date (see Figures 8.3a and 8.3b). If necessary, later verify in the *Monthly Catalog* or in the *Government Organization Manual.* Then make author card, title card (if distinctive title), and shelf list card. Remember that the number originally given to a committee or commission remains the same for its existence. It takes its identification from the president originating the body and does not change with a changing president.

In the case of Congressional committees and commissions, follow the procedure below.

Figure 8.3a

Item No. 851-J

PRESIDENT'S COMMISSION ON FINANCIAL STRUCTURE
AND REGULATIONS

General Publications   Pr37.8:F49

SL 6317; 2.22.72

Figure 8.3b

Item No. 851-J

COUNCIL ON INTERNATIONAL ECONOMICS POLICY

General Publications   Pr37.8:In8/3

SL 6316; 2.18.72

Item numbers for Congressional Committees, Commissions, and Boards. 1089.

Figure 8.4–Established Card

```
Item No. 1089

COMMISSIONS, COMMITTEES AND, BOARDS

Reports and Publications                Y3.
This item has been made for the Commissions, Com-
mittees or Boards created by Congress for specific
studies or investigations. These bodies are termin-
ated upon submission of a final report.
     For any numbers added to this check card, use
the name of the Commission for the main entry.
(UKrule)

               Depository Library No. _____

   6.7.68
```

Add a note in brackets as shown in Figure 8.4. Follow the directions for new entries as per Chapter 7. Type only information verified–i.e., item number, class number, and shipping list number and date. Then make a shelf list card. Verify the agency and series title later in appropriate sources. Complete all cards. Figures 8.5a and 8.5b are examples of further entries under the umbrella "Commissions, Committees, and Boards" of Congress.

SELECTIVE CATALOGING

Even though the major portion of the documents may be kept in a separate collection, it is almost inevitable that some will be cataloged to be integrated into the regular collection. In a smaller library, reference type material, bibliographies, or major sets may be housed in the regular stacks. In a larger library, departmental libraries will need duplicate copies for their collections.

If the documents department is to serve to its full potential, it should be the central clearinghouse for all documents in areas administered by the main library. This function is best served if the department orders all government documents, and maintains a shelf list of all holdings. This centralized function is furthered when the department, which has done the original searching for the items as a *document*, then does the searching to establish the entry as a part of the *cataloged* collection.

Figure 8.5a

```
Item No.  1089



        INTERAGENCY LAND ACQUISITION CONFERENCE

Handbooks, Manuals, Guides                    Y3.L22:8

            SL  5905;  4.1.71



May  1971 MC
```

Figure 8.5b

```
Item No.  1089



     AMERICAN REVOLUTION BICENTENNIAL COMMISSION

Bicentennial Era                        Y3.Am3/6:7-2




    Sept.  1970 MC
```

The following procedures reflect the philosophy of the documents department as the source of information on documents through acquisitions, cataloging, and record keeping. For those libraries that integrate or partially integrate their documents, the procedures described here will serve as a guide to the processing and records that should be kept even though the documents shelf list will now become merely a holdings file with cross references to the actual library location of the documents.

When a department requests a particular title for acquisition it should be sent on a properly executed order slip, according to the procedures of the library. When the order is received, specified checking steps are followed. Now the book, with its accompanying slips, is ready to be cataloged.

Basic procedures for ordering a document that is to be cataloged are described in Chapter 5. After the document has been received, the documents department must make out a multiple copy order form (see Figure 8.6) for those items ordered on vendors' forms. If the material is a serial, list each piece sent.

Figure 8.6—Multiple Copy Order Form

Class No.	AUTHOR		
List Price	TITLE		
Date Ordered			
	Edition or Series		Volumes
Date Rec'd.			
	Place	Publisher	Year
Dealer			
	Recommended by	Fund Charged	Cost
No. of Copies			
Order No.			
L.C. or Wilson Card			

Separate the forms. The white copy may be sent with the cover letter to the vendor.

The green copy is filed alphabetically with the request slip while the order is outstanding. Upon receipt of the item, payment is recorded in the space provided. When the item is sent to cataloging, mark this copy with date sent and SuDocs class number, then file this slip in the "In Catalog Dept." file. The slip is transferred to the permanent file when the buff copy is returned by the cataloging department.

Yellow and buff copies are filed with the request slip while order is outstanding. When the item is received, they are put in the book at the title page. When the cataloger receives the book, he pulls the buff card, dates and initials it, and files it in the cataloging department's "in process" file. The yellow copy is sent to the card order clerk if LC cards are to be ordered. It then holds the call number in the shelf list until permanent card is filed. When permanent cards arrive, the yellow is returned to the cataloger with the cards. The buff card is pulled from the "in process" file when the book leaves cataloging and is returned to the documents department to clear their "In Catalog Dept." file.

The pink copy is filed in the documents department order file while the order is outstanding. Upon receipt of item, payment is recorded in the space provided. Slip is attached to invoice and sent to acquisitions accountant for processing.

Basic steps in recording cataloged information are as follows: On the multiple copy order form enter call number and any changes in author or title. On shelf list card write call number, main entry, and title.

File the shelf list card by SuDocs number and the order slip by main entry, in the drawer marked "cataloging completed" (or something similar). File catalog cards in the shelf list and in the public catalog.

TRANSFERRING OR RECLASSIFYING DOCUMENTS

The library literature has recently begun to reflect a change in cataloging policies of many depository libraries. New surveys of depository collections indicate that many fully or partially integrated depository collections are being withdrawn to a separate facility using the Superintendent of Documents System.

Therefore, to provide guidelines to help handle this situation and others in which documents are being moved from one scheme to another, the following procedures have been included and described. These procedures apply to items being transferred from the integrated collection to the SuDocs collections *and* to requests for records for publications that will remain in the library's main collection.

In order to transfer or reclassify documents (to the Superintendent of Documents Classification), first, determine the classification number, main entry, and title of each item. For monographic material, fill out a request form in duplicate. A sample form is shown in Figure 8.7. Have the request approved by an appropriate person. Then, put one copy in book at title page and file the second copy by call number in "Requests for transfer" file. Write SuDocs number in upper right corner of the first page of the book. Route to head of catalog department.

Figure 8.7

For serials to be transferred or reclassified, fill out a request form (see Figure 8.8) in quadruplicate, and have it approved by an appropriate person. File one copy of the form with "Requests for transfer," and route all other forms to the head of the acquisitions department.

Figure 8.8

REQUEST FOR: (check one) Date April 13,1973

UNIVERSITY OF KENTUCKY LIBRARIES

..X... Transfer of Serial Publication*

.... Withdrawal of Serial Publication*

Call No. ....973.3:..Am35.

Author ....

Title American state papers

Volumes, editions, and/or years ....all

Transfer from: ...Stacks. TO: GPD

Check, if appropriate: Declassify ......X. Current issues only ....

Requested by: .GPD. Approved .... Acquisitions .... Cataloging ....

(* Send 1st three slips to Ass't. Director, Pub. Services. Do not execute transfer or discard materials until yellow slip is returned to you.) SuDocs Z1.1

Review both serial and monographic materials returned from the catalog department. Arrange catalog cards returned (i.e., all main entry cards, shelf list cards, etc.) together in proper order. Be sure all items represented on cards are returned. Erase all call numbers from books and mark with Superintendent of Documents numbers. Make Superintendent of Documents cards for the documents collection.

For publications which will remain in departmental collections, make SuDocs shelf list cards. For numbered and dated publications (Figure 8.9) type Dewey or LC number in upper left corner and type SuDocs number in usual place (if possible).

For cuttered publications (Figure 8.10) type Dewey or LC number in margin opposite title. Enter main entry per LC, title, and Cutter number after date.

File returned catalog cards for books returned to documents collection by Dewey or LC number in "Transferred" file. File returned catalog cards for books remaining in a departmental collection in the department's public catalog.

WEEDING

Document collections, just like other collections, often find that more space is needed and that some older publications have lost their appeal and/or usefulness. The Superintendent of Documents has specified that:

Figure 8.9

Phys.Lib. 528 Un3	U.S. Naval Observatory. American ephemeris and nautical almanac.					D213.8		
1951	1961	1971	1981	1991	2001	2011	2021	
1952	1962	1972	1982	1992	2002	2012	2022	
1953	1963	1973	1983	1993	2003	2013	2023	
1954 Supp	1964	1974	1984	1994	2004	2014	2024	
1955	1965	1975	1985	1995	2005	2015	2025	
1956	1966	1976	1986	1996	2006	2016	2026	
1957	1967	1977	1987	1997	2007	2017	2027	
1958	1968	1978	1988	1998	2008	2018	2028	
1959	1969	1979	1989	1999	2009	2019	2029	
1960	1970	1980	1990	2000	2010	2020	2030	

Library Form No. 21B

Figure 8.10

LC2.8　U.S. Library of Congress. General Reference
　　　　　and Bibliography Division.
　　　　　Manuals.

Lib.Scl.　　Haviland, Virginia.
016.80989　　Children's literature, a guide to
H299　　reference sources. 1966. (C43)

All depository libraries *not* served by designated regional depository *must retain permanently* one copy of all government publications received under depository distribution, except superseded publications or those issued later in bound form or microfacsimile form . . .

Depositories which *are* served by regional depositories may dispose of publications which they have retained for at least 5 years with the permission of and in accordance with instructions from the regional depository which serves their area.[1]

The only exception made to the above regulations is the substitution of micro-facsimile materials for any holdings, provided that the microfacsimile copies are accessible and the necessary reading equipment is available.[2] For a more complete discussion of the regulations concerning the weeding of depository materials, see the publication *Instructions to Depository Libraries*, which is distributed to all depositories by the Superintendent of Documents.

Unfortunately for the librarian, the main problem involved in weeding is the lack of current guidelines available for determining which materials in the collection will be of lasting importance. Therefore, the decision to discard must be based upon a personal knowledge of user needs, just as the decision concerning which depository items to receive is made today by selective depositories. One saving note is the growing availability of government publications in microformat, which will allow little-used items to be discarded without loss of valuable information.

Suggested procedures for weeding are as follows: For general depository items, check the depository date stamped on the front cover or inside on the title page of the publication to make certain that the publication has been held at least five years. Then, remove the publication to the work area and mark it and the shelf list card *withdrawn*. Mark the number of publications withdrawn in the superseded/withdrawn column of the "Items Handled Sheet" (see Chapter 6, Counting). Write to the regional depository library describing the material to be withdrawn and requesting instructions. Dispose of the publications according to the instructions received from the regional depository library.

For depository materials superseded by microfacsimile materials, the procedures are the same as that for handling general depository publications except that the five-year waiting period need not be observed and the shelf list card should be marked microfacsimile only.

For non-depository materials, courtesy treatment is preferred. First, follow procedures for general depository items. Then, write to the regional depository library describing the materials available for distribution. If the regional depository library wants the materials or knows of a library that wants the materials, mail to the requester. If the regional library does not need the materials (or does not offer names of libraries that do), discard them.

BINDING

Acceptance of depository status entails proper maintenance and care of the collection. Bound volumes are easier to handle and to shelve. While the depository law says nothing about requirements for binding, it seems more practical to bind documents according to the overall policy of the library. Because of the volume of materials involved, special procedures and records for binding must be developed.

Each library will have its own internal procedures with requirements for number of copies of bindery slips, etc. But certain very broad procedures can be formulated that may prove of value.

A master pattern for binding serials eliminates errors in transcribing. When this pattern is duplicated to provide as many copies as necessary, all basic information is transferred. There remains, then, only to type identification for the specific volume to be bound.

This "Binding Pattern" file contains samples that give the exact wording, pattern, cover color, print color, frequency of binding, and special instructions for all serial titles bound by the library. These master cards should be filed by an appropriate system—i.e., by call number, alphabetically by agency, alphabetically by title, or some other. These cards can be made all at once when there is extra time available, or the file may be built as needed.

When the book is returned from the bindery, examine the spine to be sure that the pattern was followed exactly. But be sure also to check the inside of the publication to determine that the contents are in correct order.

Finally, the charge card may be pulled, binding slip discarded, and the bound volume shelved.

Some publications will require only mending or inexpensive binding. These materials are usually handled by library staff.

Details for commercial binding, cheap binding and home library binding are considered below.

Commercial Binding

Serials

Specifications for binding serials: Maintain a permanent binding pattern file for all serials. This pattern (see Figure 8.11) should provide the following data for each title: a) name of department, b) color of binding, c) color of lettering, d) volume and date pattern, e) name of agency, f) title, g) classification number, h) special instructions (if they will apply to all volumes to be bound), and any other information necessary.

To prepare the volume for binding, arrange the material in the exact order it should appear in the book and tie together in one stack.

Prepare the binding slips by photocopying the pattern, having three copies for each volume to be sent. Fill in the copies with exact information for the volume in hand. Add any special instructions necessary. Date the binding slips with the date of bindery pickup. Arrange the slips in three stacks with one copy of the binding slip in the first issue of the volume, one copy attached to the overlay of charge card (for circulation records), and one copy separate.

Make out charge card with date sent to the bindery and file it in the regular circulation file. Add to statistics sheet as explained in Counting Section of Chapter 6.

When a new title has to be bound, make a new binding pattern and follow procedures outlined above.

For an old title that is new to the bindery, make a rub of the spine of the volume. Place the rub with the binding slip in the front of the book and follow procedures outlined above.

Figure 8.11–Serials Binding Pattern

UNIVERSITY OF KENTUCKY LIBRARIES
Division: Government, Publications

U.S. National Aeronautics
and
Space Administration

Scientic and Technical
Aerospace Reports

NAS1.9
4

SPINE LETTERING
follow wording and arrangement
given above

vol. date pattern:

color
no.   588

___ new title
     lettering: _x_ gold
                ___ white
                ___ black
_x_ repeat
___ rub enclosed
___ bind as is
___ strip to pub. vol.

COVERS:
___ remove
___ bind in all

ADS:
___ remove
___ leave in

INDEX:
___ in front
___ in back
_x_ bind without

special instructions
Remove all indexes from
semi-monthly issues and bind
text only. Bind table of
contents at front of volume.

Remove table of contents
from individual issues and
bind in front of volume.

volume date pattern:
1 __vol. x__
2 __nos.x-x__
3 __mo.-mo.__
4 __19xx__
5 _____
6 _____
7 _____

Monographs

Procedures for binding monographs are different from those for serials because the binding pattern must be determined for each item at the time the decision to bind is made. In this case it is best to use the form supplied by bindery (usually a multiple copy). (See Figure 8.12 for sample.) Make three copies filling in space for cloth and ink colors. If there is no great preference, leave color spaces blank. This allows bindery to make use of extra materials and lowers prices. If there are no special instructions, mark "Bind complete." Identify the item on the form by listing the agency, title, and classification number. Date the slip with the date of bindery pickup and follow directions given for serials regarding disposition of copies of the binding slip, charging out and statistics.

Cheap Binding

This type of binding, sometimes called "perfect" binding, has several limitations. It will not withstand the wear and tear of sewn, buckram binding. Instead, the cover is glued to the spine, and the remainder of the book is covered with cloth. It can be used only for books which have been previously sewn together and is limited to books of certain size and thickness, i.e., a maximum of 3/4" thick for books fairly heavily used and 2" for books less used or a minimum of 32 pages. Usually the color of the binding cannot be specified. Perfect binding should not be used for serials or monographs in series. Because of the size limitations, the identification of the volume is lengthwise on the spine and often the shortened name of the agency and title may not be completely clear. Furthermore, the classification number is not easily read at this position and angle.

If complete identification of the volume is not given on title page, write it there and enclose in parentheses. Write classification number on the verso. Then, to prepare volume for binding, indicate the author with a line under the first letter of the first word of the agency. Be certain that the classification number is on the back of the title page. If the paper cover is the only title page, photocopy it and attach a note, "Bind in photocopied page as title page." Make three copies of a 3 x 5" slip which lists name of library, name of agency (i.e., author), title, and classification number. State preference for cloth or vinyl cover and give date of bindery shipment. Then follow general directions above for charging out, disposition of forms, and statistics.

Home Library Binding

Prepare serials according to instructions for commercial binding and monographs according to instructions for cheap binding. Attach a slip which lists classification number, title, type of binder (i.e., pamphlet or string), and documents department notation. Charge out as for any other circulation and send to Bindery Preparations Department.

When the material is returned, check to see that instructions were followed. Type a slip (see Figure 8.13) and paste it to the front cover. On this slip list agency, title, and the exact pieces of a serial. Label with classification number in upper left corner of the front cover, stamp the cover and discard charge card.

Figure 8.12—Binding Pattern (Monograph or Serial
Bound as Monograph)

ART GUILD BINDERY, Inc.

Order No._____

July 7, 1970

PLEASE CHECK INFORMATION BELOW

Name of Library	LIBRARY UNIVERSITY OF KENTUCKY	Government Publications Department
		Dept.

| New Title ☒ | Color No. | Split into Two Volumes |
| Repeat ☐ | **193** | if too heavy ☐ |

| Rub: Enclosed ☐ Make New ☐ | Letter Spine Exactly As Shown Below Indicating Title, Vol. No., Year, Date, Part No., Call No., and Imprints if Desired. |

Bind as is ☒

**U.S.
Congress**

Title Page and Contents:

Separate ☐
Not pub. ☐   Stub for ☐
Bind Without ☐

**House of
Representatives**

Index:

Bind in Front ☐   in Back ☐
Bind Without ☐
Stub for ☐   Not pub. ☐

**Committee on
Un-American
Activities**

Covers:

Remove ☒   Bind in all ☐
Bind in First Cover Only ☐
Bind in Front Covers Only ☐

**Cumulative
Index to
Publications
1938-54**

Ads:

Remove ☐   Leave In ☐
Remove, through
paged in, if without text ☐

**Y4.Un1^2
In2**

Parts or Supplements:

Bind in Place ☐
Bind in Back of Vol. ☐

Imprint: Yes ☐   No ☐

Special Instructions:

Figure 8.13

```
┌─────────────────────────────────────┐
│                                      │
│                                      │
│        U. S. Census Bureau           │
│                                      │
│   Current Population Reports         │
│                                      │
│      Population Estimates            │
│                                      │
│         Nos. 260-310                 │
│                                      │
│                                      │
└─────────────────────────────────────┘
```

CIRCULATION

"Depository libraries shall make Government publications available for the free use of the general public."[3] This is the requirement as set forth in 44 USC 1911. Most libraries interpret the law to mean that depository materials are intended for circulation and use on the same basis as commercially published books and periodicals purchased by the library. This means that some depository items may be treated as rare books, or as reference tools and never be circulated outside the library. Or they may be put on temporary reserve as a result of particularly heavy usage.

If the library has chosen to have a partially or completely integrated collection, there could be no easy way to indicate to circulation staff which books could be charged.

This manual has assumed a separate collection. In such cases, when the materials are housed apart from the rest of the collections, the Documents Department should circulate materials according to its own requirements. This makes it necessary to record circulation statistics and general reference service supplied by the department.

FOOTNOTES

[1] U.S. Superintendent of Documents. *Instructions to Depository Libraries.* (Washington, GPO, 1967), pp. 11-12.
[2] *Ibid.*
[3] *Ibid.*

Chapter 9

CATALOGING AND CLASSIFYING
BY OTHER SYSTEMS

In 1951, Anne Markley wrote, "The recording and indexing of government publications has been a source of conflicting opinions, diverse practices, and genuine bewilderment for a longer time than any of us can remember."[1] Unfortunately, over 20 years later this statement is still painfully true. The absence of any universal guidelines that can be applied uniformly to the organization of government publications is a well-known fact.

The disadvantages of the Superintendent of Documents Cataloging and Classification System (see Chapter 2) cause many small libraries and a few large ones to seek other ways of organizing these materials. The most common systems used at this time include 1) subject classification (by Library of Congress or Dewey) using established Library of Congress entries; 2) alphabetizing materials by government organization title; or 3) adopting homemade or especially designed systems.

It is not the purpose of this manual to elaborate upon systems other than that of the Superintendent of Documents. Brief mention of them, however, will give the reader an idea of the differences and similarities that exist. Suggestions for further reading are given in the bibliography in the appendix for those who desire to pursue the subject further with an eye to utilization of any one or any combinations. Within the text of this manual we have made note of differences in processing that would result from the partial integration of the documents into the library's general collection. No matter what scheme is finally used by the library, many of the principles suggested in the preceding chapters will still apply, as will most of the records.

First, to reiterate the principles of the SuDocs system. It uses the corporate agency as main entry, and not the individual who might have been responsible for its writing. Prior to September 1947, it used the major department with bureau division as the identifying body; since that time, it has used direct entry. It identifies a publication by the name of the agency at the time the work was authorized (there seems to be a current tendency to violate this rule, as with the 1970 Decennial Census). Certainly one of its most striking features is its use of the inverted order of the agency name. The shelf arrangement is archival, and its classification scheme was devised to serve as a finding tool.

SUBJECT CATALOGING AND CLASSIFICATION
BY LC OR DEWEY

The alternative system most often discussed and used is the subject cataloging of documents as represented by Library of Congress or Dewey Classifications. To explain and illustrate this subject system in its entirety would be pointless and would take a separate book; however, a brief discussion of the subject cataloging system as it applies to federal publications is necessary.

One of the reasons for the popularity of subject cataloging and classification for documents is that it shelves those documents with other publications on the same topic. This means that the patron or user of the collection need use only one index to determine what books are available on his topic. This advantage proves elusive, however, when one closely examines the nature of federal publications.

Federal publications are generally issued in series. Many of these publications are then classified by LC as a series and each individual publication receives only limited, if any, treatment in the card catalog. Also, although series publications deal generally with the same subject area, with government documents this is not always so; the result is that publications dealing with widely diverse topics will be shelved not with other books on the same topic but with their series.

Using subject classification and cataloging also brings to the fore the problem of entries. LC cataloging rules call for government entries to be established by the legal name of the government agency. This leads to a mass of confusing author entries beginning U.S. Department of . . ., Bureau of . . ., Division of . . ., etc. Thus, for the patron it is easier not to use the card catalog at all than to wade through hundreds of meaningless entries.

Nor, in fact, can the uninitiated always decide whether an institution is an official organ. Cross references to changes in names of agencies frequently give no hint as to the dates of such bodies. Inclusion of dates of existence and changes would make the information much more accessible.

Another major argument against the exclusive use of LC classification and cataloging is the time lag in processing government publications. The volume of publications from the federal government—*17,000* to *20,000* items a year are now listed in the *Monthly Catalog* alone—and the low priority that federal publications have in LC processing[2] make it impossible to handle federal publications in this way without incurring huge backlogs or tremendous expense in original cataloging. Having said this, then, one may characterize other systems as using essentially the same philosophy of classification. They approach a collection by its governmental author and assume that the purpose of the organization will, to some extent at least, present a subject arrangement.

Finally, the reduction in usefulness of the *Monthly Catalog* and similar governmental indexes along with the other disadvantages of subject cataloging have forced many libraries to use the system only on a selective basis.

A note about the processing and records within this system must be made at this time. Even if a library selects full subject integration into the library collection, the general process described in this manual could apply. Some separate control of what has and has not been received on depository is necessitated by federal law. Thus, the processes suggested here would be carried out, while one further step—cataloging—would be added. Procedures for selective cataloging have been presented in Chapter 8, and the principles described will serve as a guide even for full cataloging.

ALPHABETIZING BY AUTHOR

At the present time, the third most accepted and generally known method for handling documents is alphabetizing by governmental author. With a smaller collection, this arrangement is rather easily managed; however, the effort required to catalog and classify large collections in this way is cumbersome and extremely difficult.

To use this system, one must have some form of departmentalized collection. Its arrangement is primarily by issuing agency, using key words of the name without the use of notation.

Obviously, the first decision must be to decide whether offices are to be entered directly under their own names or as subordinates of departments and large independent bodies. Generally, the practice seems to enter and arrange the publications of an agency having autonomous status—bureau, office, service, authority, survey, administration, commission, etc.—directly under its own name rather than that of its parent body. (For example, Office of Management and Budget, not Executive Office of the President, is the key identification.) This same principle is followed for independent agencies and quasi-governmental bodies. Bureau of American Ethnology (no longer in existence) and Freer Gallery of Art are not first identified through their connection with the Smithsonian Institution.

In addition to filing under a word that suggests the agencies' subject specialty, this alphabetical subject arrangement has the advantages of bringing together on the shelves many publications in the same or related subject areas.

The publications of a division or other non-autonomous unit whose subject is dependent upon the structure of the superior agency should be so arranged by the significant word of the division that they form a secondary arrangement under that main body. This rather labored procedure is an attempt to group materials by subject, because the average library user is looking either for a title or for information on a given subject, and not for the entire output of a branch of government.

The difficulty of deciding which place an agency will hold in the total arrangement is compounded by another purely physical task. Imagine the manhours involved in underlining, or bracketing, or writing in all the elements necessary for identifying one particular piece among all others—not to mention difficulty of shelving and reshelving each time, as the document is searched for the elusive marks.

Within this system, the records for federal documents that must be maintained are essentially the same as the records under the SuDocs classification scheme. In this case, the entries are those of the local library instead of those established by the Library of the Public Documents Division, and the shelf list is arranged alphabetically by these entries. Of course, this change alone will modify the usefulness of the shipping lists and *Monthly Catalog*, and will complicate the shelf listing procedures; however, many of the principles presented in the processing chapters of this manual will remain essentially the same.

The effort involved in cataloging, classifying, and servicing a large collection now staggers those who have inherited this alphabetically arranged mass of government output. The magnitude of this operation, however, has been ignored by more than one documents department, and projects now exist for transferring documents.

SWANK, JACKSON, AND PLAIN "J" CLASSIFICATION SCHEMES

In some libraries, the classification scheme selected for use has been the result of a decision to integrate all government publications—local, state, federal, and international—into one system. Since there are no widely accepted schemes for doing this, homemade or locally created systems have been adopted. Examples of two well-known schemes of this type are those developed by Raynard Swank and Ellen Jackson.

Raynard Swank defined a set of filing rules that incorporated all government publications. It is based on a vertical division by issuing office rather than a horizontal division by subject. He identifies each state and country with an arabic numeral. This immediately presents a major problem. Since he first introduced his concept, two states (Alaska and Hawaii) have been added to the United States. Either his previously alphabetical arrangement must be interrupted, or he must renumber the entire state collection. He assigned certain numbers to other nations of the world. To some extent, this has a political or geographic significance. A proliferation of new nations, however, has presented the problem of integrating their publications logically with others.

The next element of his scheme assigns a Cutter number for the agency or issuing office. Now the problem arises: How do you Cutter the offerings of the many levels of government that begin with "Department," "Office," "Bureau," etc., or the name of the state, or which form of the several names of some of the organizations do you choose? He suggests the first distinctive word. But we have "Public Welfare," "Public Health," etc.

Publication numbers are assigned to types or series according to the principles envisioned by the SuDocs system. But while this arrangement began with an alphabetic list of the bureaus then in existence, and continues now with chronological numbering as they are established, Mr. Swank has provided no key to the structure of the several states. Apparently he did not intend this system to be applied to federal documents.[3]

Miss Ellen Jackson developed a notation system that can be used for classifying documents of federal, state, municipal, and international bodies. It is not a class scheme, but a system that can be applied to any arrangement that the library decides to use. Based on an arrangement by issuing office, it consolidates (by code and alphabetically by agency), all offices dealing with a particular field—e.g., mining.

In 1946, this system had 11 main classes. Book, volume, and issue numbering followed, in general, conventional library usage. It allowed all publications to be filed into one collection, which cannot conveniently be done when other systems of government documents organization are used. But a number had to be supplied from a schedule and could not be taken from the shipping list, the *Monthly Catalog*, or other familiar source. The classifying was not mechanical; it was necessary to use judgment in identifying by word or agency. It was not widely used, so interlibrary cooperation of any kind was limited.[4]

The records for federal documents that are necessary under the systems of Mr. Swank and Miss Jackson are generally the same as the records for a library with a departmentalized documents collection using the Superintendent of Documents classification. The notations are different and the entries reflect local cataloging; however, order forms, shelf list cards, and item number cards remain essential and essentially the same. Main entry and title files under this system would now seem to be a necessity, since the *Monthly Catalog* could no longer serve as the only link between the user and the shelves (some manner of cross references would have to be developed). The specialized technical processes associated with federal documents would still have to be managed to maintain control over the federal collection and all "housekeeping" or optional processes would change only as far as the notation system required a change.

Of course, other systems are being developed to cope with the problems associated with government publications, especially the publications of the federal government. Some libraries have suggested that departmentalized or separated document collections move to a modification of the Library of Congress "J" class.[5] Others suggest still different possibilities.

The continuous rise in the cost of the cataloging process and the increasing sophistication and availability of centrally published indexes are leading more and more research and general libraries—public as well as academic—with large holdings of government documents to consider the use of the standard documents classification in a departmentalized collection.

These various forms of classification and shelving may use one of three types of corporate entry: 1) The direct entry presents the legal name of the agency responsible for a publication. Frequently difficulties arise here because no one knows the legal name. Legislation that establishes it may sometimes refer to it by another name in later appropriations. 2) The inverted name (of an agency which begins with a generic term followed by a preposition) is used in order to place the significant noun at the beginning of the entry instead of in its normal position. 3) A truncated heading is often a descriptive or popular name rather than a legal one.

The point to keep in mind is that documents classification and records should be designed to serve the policy and preferences of the library (within the structure required by federal law) and to aid in the reference and service of the collection.

FOOTNOTES

[1] Anne E. Markley, *Library Records for Government Publications*, (Berkeley, University of California Press, 1951), p. 1.

[2] "L.C. Practice with Regard to U.S. Documents," in *Library Resources and Technical Services* 14:609-610 (Fall 1970).

[3] Raynard Swank, "A Classification for State, County, and Municipal Documents," in *Special Libraries* 35: (April 1944).

[4] Ellen Pauline Jackson, "A Notation for a Public Documents Classification," in *Oklahoma A.&M. College Bulletin*, No. 8, 1946.

[5] Mina Pease, "The Plain "J": A Documents Classification System," in *Library Resources and Technical Services* 16:315-25 (Summer 1972).

BIBLIOGRAPHY

GENERAL WORKS

Boyd, Anne M. *United States Government Publications.* 3rd ed. rev. by Rae E. Ripps. New York, H. W. Wilson, 1949. 627p.

Caldwell, George. "University Libraries and Government Publications: A Survey," *College and Research Libraries* 22:30-34 (January 1961).

Documents to the People, Volume 1– . 1972– . Quarterly. Issued by ALA's Government Documents Round Table.

Federal Depository Library Service in New York State: A Report by the State Library Committee on Federal Depository Service. Albany, N.Y., The University of the State of New York, The State Education Department, The New York State Library, 1964.

"Federal, State and Local Government Publications," *Library Trends* 15:1 (July 1966). (Entire issue.)

Fry, Bernard M., and others. *Research Design for a Comprehensive Study of the Use, Bibliographic Control, and Distribution of Government Publications.* Washington, U.S. Office of Education, Bureau of Research, 1970.

Government Publications Review. Elmsford, N.Y., Microforms International Marketing Corp., 1973– . Quarterly.

Holzbauer, H. "Bibliographic Organization in the Federal Government," *Wilson Library Bulletin* 40:719-720+ (April 1966).

Kling, Robert E., Jr. *The Government Printing Office.* New York, Praeger Publishers, Inc., 1970.

Leavitt, Edward. "Government Publications in the University Library," *Library Journal* 86:1741-1743 (May 1, 1961).

McReynolds, Helen. *Microforms of United States Government Publications.* Urbana, Graduate School of Library Science, University of Illinois, 1963. (Occasional Paper No. 69.)

Morehead, Joe. "U.S. Government Documents: A Mazeway Miscellany." Column in *RQ* (beginning with Volume 7, No. 3, Spring 1968).

Problems of Regional Depository Libraries: A Panel Discussion Held at Syracuse University on June 9, 1966. Albany, N.Y., The University of the State of New York, The State Education Department, The New York State Library, 1967.

"The Question of Inversion," *Monthly Catalog*, No. 210 (June 1912), pp. 821-823.

Schmeckebier, Laurence F., and Roy B. Eastin. *Government Publications and Their Use.* 2nd rev. ed. Washington, Brookings Institution, 1969.

Shore, Philip. "An Evaluation of U.S. Document Bibliography," *Library Resources and Technical Services* 4:34-43 (Winter 1960).

U.S. Congress. House. Committee on Government Operations. *Federal Statutes on the Availability of Information.* Committee Print. Washington, GPO, 1960.

U.S. Congress. House. Committee on House Administration. *Revision of Depository Library Laws.* Hearings before Subcommittee to Study Federal Printing and Paperwork. 85th Cong., 1st sess., 1958.

U.S. Congress. Joint Committee on Printing. *Government Depository Libraries.* Joint Committee Print. Washington, GPO, 1970.

U.S. Superintendent of Documents. *An Explanation of the Superintendent of Documents Classification System.* Washington, GPO, 1970.

BIBLIOGRAPHIES AND INDEXES

American Historical Association. *General Index to Papers and Annual Reports of the AHA, 1884-1914.* Washington, Smithsonian Institution, 1918. 2v.

Ames, John Griffith. *Comprehensive Index to the Publications of the United States Government, 1881-1893.* Washington, GPO, 1905. 2v.

Andriot, Jeanne K., and John L. Andriot. *Checklist and Index of Congressional Hearings, 1958-1960.* McLean, Va., Documents Index, 1967.

Andriot, John L. *Guide to U.S. Government Serials and Periodicals.* McLean, Va., Documents Index, 1962– . Annual.

Andriot, John L. *Guide to U.S. Government Statistics.* 3rd ed. Revised and enlarged. Arlington, Va., Documents Index, 1961.

Bibliography-Index to Current U.S. JPRS Translations. New York, Research and Microfilm Publications, CCM Information Corporation, Inc., 1962– .

Body, Alexander C. *Annotated Bibliography of Bibliographies on Government Publications.* Kalamazoo, Mich., the author, 1967. Supplements, 1968 and 1970.

Brown, Kenneth R. *PB to AD/ATI Number Correlation Index.* Los Angeles, Garret Corporation, 1967.

CIS/Index: Congressional Information Service/Index to the Publications of the United States Congress. Washington, Congressional Information Service, 1969– . Monthly (with quarterly and annual cumulations).

Childs, James B. "United States of America Official Publications," *Annals of Library Science* 9:84-91 (June 1962).

Commerce Clearing House. *Congressional Index: The Week in Congress.* Chicago, 1937– . Weekly.

ERIC Educational Documents Index, 1966-1969. New York, CCM, 1970-1971.

Flessher, Laura. *American Minorities: A Checklist of Bibliographies Published by Government Agencies, 1960-1970.* Sacramento, California State Library, 1970.

Foster, D. L. *Checklist of U.S. Government Publications in the Arts.* Urbana, Graduate School of Library Science, University of Illinois, 1969.

Government Reference Books: A Biennial Guide to U.S. Government Publications. Comp. by Sally Wynkoop. Littleton, Colo., Libraries Unlimited, 1970– . Biennial.

Government Reports Announcements and *Government Reports Index.* Springfield, Va., NTIS, 1946– . Semi-monthly.

Grassroots of America and a Computerized Index to the American State Papers: Land Grants and Claims (1789-1837) with Other Aids to Research. (Government document serial set numbers 28 through 36.) Edited by Phillip W. McMullin. Salt Lake City, Utah, Gendex Corporation, 1972.

Greely, Adolphus W. *Public Documents of the First Fourteen Congresses, 1789-1817.* Washington, GPO, 1900. Supplement, 1903.

Hasse, Adelaide R. *Index to U.S. Documents Relating to Foreign Affairs, 1828-61.* Washington, Carnegie Institution, 1914-1921. (Publication No. 185.)

Herner, Saul. *A Brief Guide to Sources of Scientific and Technical Information.* Washington, Information Resources Press, 1969.

Herner, Saul, and Jeanne Moody. *Exhibits of Sources of Scientific and Technical Information.* Washington, Information Resources Press, 1971.

Index to Readex Microprint Edition of JPRS Reports (Joint Publications Research Service), Oct. 1958-Dec. 1963. Prepared by Mary Elizabeth Poole. New York, Readex Microprint Corporation, 1964? _____, *1964-1966.* Prepared by Louise J. Hawkins. New York, Readex Microprint Corporation, 1967? _____, *1967-1970.* Prepared by Louise J. Hawkins. New York, Readex Microprint Corporation, 1971?

Jackson, Ellen. *Subject Guide to Major United States Government Publications.* Chicago, American Library Association, 1968.

Kilty, Theresa. "Government Publications for School and Public Libraries," *Kentucky Library Association Bulletin* 36:18-22 (April 1972).

Kiraldi, L. "Some Problems: Selecting Government Periodicals: With a List of Government Periodicals Indexed by Abstracting and Indexing Sources," *RQ* 7:166-169 (Summer 1968).

Klempner, Irving M. *Diffusion of Abstracting and Indexing Sources for Government-Sponsored Research.* Metuchen, N.J., Scarecrow Press, 1968.

Koch, Annalise K., and Mary Elizabeth Poole. *Named Subcommittees of the United States Congress 1941-1969.* McLean, Va., Documents Index, 1970.

Kyriak, Theodore E. *JPRS Catalog Cards in Book Form.* Annapolis, Md., Research and Microfilm Publications, 1957/61-1968. New York, CCM Information Corporation, 1969– .

Kyriak, Theodore E. *Subject Index to U.S. Joint Publications Research Service Translations.* Annapolis, Md., Research and Microfilm Publications, 1966-1967. New York, CCM Information Corporation, 1968– .

Leidy, W. Philip. *A Popular Guide to Government Publications.* 3rd ed. New York, Columbia University Press, 1968.

Lester, M. A. *Federal and State Government Publications of Professional Interest to the School Librarian: A Bibliographical Essay.* Urbana, Graduate School of Library Science, University of Illinois, 1971. (Occasional Papers, No. 100.)

Mason, John Brown. *Research Resources: Annotated Guide to the Social Sciences. V. 2, Official Publications: U.S. Government, United Nations, International Organizations and Statistical Sources.* Santa Barbara, Calif., ABC-Clio Press, 1971.

Massachusetts Institute of Technology Libraries. *Correlation Index to Current Department of Defense Research Reports.* Cambridge, Mass., M.I.T. Press, 1963.

Mechanic, Sylvia. *Annotated List of Selected United States Government Publications Available to Depository Libraries.* New York, H. W. Wilson, 1971.

Nakata, Yuri. *A Guide to Selected United States Government Publications: Especially for Students of History and Political Science.* Chicago, University of Illinois at Chicago Circle Library, 1970.

Namias, Jean. *Handbook of Selected Sample Surveys in the Federal Government, with Annotated Bibliography 1960-1968.* New York, St. John's University Press, 1969.

O'Hara, Frederic J. "Selected Government Publications—Reference Books and Other Worthwhile Titles," *Wilson Library Bulletin*, March 1969–Dec. 1973.

Pestana, Harold R. *Bibliography of Congressional Geology.* New York, Hafner Publishing Company, Inc., 1972.

Plischke, Elmer. *American Foreign Relations: A Bibliography of Official Sources.* College Park, Md., Bureau of Governmental Research, College of Business and Public Administration, University of Maryland, 1955.

Pohle, Linda C. *A Guide to Popular Government Publications: For Libraries and Home Reference.* Littleton, Colo., Libraries Unlimited, 1972.

Poore, Benjamin Perley. *A Descriptive Catalogue of the Government Publications of the United States, September 5, 1774–March 4, 1881.* Washington, GPO, 1885.

Rawson, N. "For the Businessman Engaged in Foreign Trade: A Guide to Foreign Trade Publications of the U.S. Government," *Special Libraries* 59:447-451 (July 1968).

Research in Education. Washington, Office of Education, 1966– . Monthly.

Schreiber, M. F. *Classified and Annotated Bibliography of U.S. Government Publications in Literature and Literary Criticism, 1945-1970, with a Discussion of the Issuing Agencies.* (Research Paper). Kent, Ohio, Kent State University, 1971.

Schwarzkopf, LeRoy. "U.S. Government Publications." Column in *Booklist.*

Scientific and Technical Aerospace Reports (STAR). Washington, NASA, 1963– . Semi-monthly.

Smith, Clifford Neal. *Federal Land Series: A Calendar of Archival Materials on the Land Patents Issued by the U.S. Government with Subject, Tract, and Name Indexes.* Chicago, ALA, 1972. 2v.

U.S. Air Force Department. *When to Buy What: A Buying Calendar for Annual Publications.* San Francisco, Pacific Air Force, 1971. (PACAF Basic Bibliographies.)

U.S. Library of Congress. *Non-GPO Imprints Received in the Library of Congress, July 1967 through December 1969.* Washington, LC, 1970. _____ . _____ . *Non-GPO Imprints Received in the Library of Congress.* Washington, LC, 1971– . Annual.

U.S. Superintendent of Documents. *Catalog of the Public Documents of Congress and of All Departments of the Government of the United States.* Washington, GPO, 1896-1940. (Known as *Document Catalog.*)

U.S. Superintendent of Documents. *Checklist of United States Public Documents, 1789-1909.* 3rd ed., rev. and enl. Washington, GPO, 1911.

U.S. Superintendent of Documents. *Checklist of United States Public Documents, 1789-1970: Indexes.* Comp. by Daniel and Marilyn Lester. Washington, United States Historical Documents Institute, 1972. 5v.

U.S. Superintendent of Documents. *Inactive and Discontinued Items from the 1950 Revision of the Classified List.* Washington, GPO, rev. July 15, 1958.

U.S. Superintendent of Documents. *Index to the Reports and Documents of Congress.* Washington, GPO, 1895-1933. (Known as *Document Index.*)

U.S. Superintendent of Documents. *List of Classes of United States Government Publications Available for Selection by Depository Libraries.* Washington, GPO. Annual.

U.S. Superintendent of Documents. *Monthly Catalog of United States Government Publications.* Washington, GPO, 1895– . Monthly.

U.S. Superintendent of Documents. *Monthly Catalog of United States Government Publications, 1895-1924.* Washington, Carrollton Press, 1974– . (In progress.)

U.S. Superintendent of Documents. *Monthly Catalog: Cumulative Subject Index, 1900-1971.* Washington, Carrollton Press, 1973– . (In progress.)

U.S. Superintendent of Documents. *Monthly Catalog: Cumulative Personal Author Index, 1941-1970.* Ann Arbor, Mich., Pierian Press, 1971-1972.

U.S. Superintendent of Documents. *Numerical Lists and Schedule of Volumes of the Reports and Documents of Congress.* Washington, GPO, 1934— . Annual.

U.S. Superintendent of Documents. *Price Lists.* Washington, GPO, 1898— . Irregular.

U.S. Superintendent of Documents. *Selected U.S. Government Publications.* Washington, GPO, 1928— . Biweekly.

U.S. Superintendent of Documents. *Tables of and Annotated Index to the Congressional Series of United States Public Documents.* Washington, GPO, 1902.

Vinge, Clarence L., and A. G. Vinge. *U.S. Government Publications for Research and Teaching in Geography and Related Social and Natural Sciences.* Totowa, N.J., Littlefield, Adams and Co., 1967.

White, Thomas M. *Guide to United States-JPRS Research Translations, 1957-1966.* Annapolis, Md., Research and Microfilm Publications, 1966.

Wilcox, Jerome Kear. *United States Reference Publications: A Guide to the Current Reference Publications of the Federal Government.* Boston, F. W. Faxon Co., 1931. Supplement, 1932.

Wisdom, Donald F. "Significant Publications: U.S. Government Publications," *RQ* 7:126-128 (Spring 1966).

Wisdom, Donald F., and William P. Kilroy. *Popular Names of U.S. Government Reports: A Catalog.* 2nd ed. Washington, GPO, 1970.

Wood, Jennings. *United States Government Publications: A Partial List of Non-GPO Imprints.* Chicago, American Library Association, 1964.

Wynar, Christine L. "Government Publications," *School Media Quarterly*, Fall 1973— .

Wynkoop, Sally. *Subject Guide to Government Reference Books.* Littleton, Colo., Libraries Unlimited, 1972.

Wynkoop, Sally, and David W. Parish. *Directories of Government Agencies.* Rochester, N.Y., Libraries Unlimited, 1969.

TECHNICAL PROCESSES

Barr, William F. "Advantages and Disadvantages of the Superintendent of Documents Classification As a Key to a Depository Collection," *College and Research Libraries* 12:40-42 (January 1951).

Bird, Viola, and others. *Order Procedures: A Manual.* No. 2. South Hackensack, N.J., Rothman, 1960. (AALL Publications Series, No. 2).

Boylan, Nancy G. "Identifying Technical Reports through U.S. Government Reports and Its Published Indexes," *College and Research Libraries* 28:175-183 (May 1967).

California State Library, Government Publications Section. *U.S. Government Publications: Acquisition, Processing and Use.* Proceedings of three workshops. Edited by Elizabeth Howes and Mary Schell. Sacramento, 1967.

Clarke, N. F. "Cataloging, Classification and Storage of Government Publications When Incorporated into the General Library Collection," *Library Trends* 15:58-71 (July 1966).

Committee on Scientific and Technical Information. Federal Council for Science and Technology. *Standard for Descriptive Cataloging of Government Scientific and Technical Reports.* Rev. 1. Washington, 1966. (PB 173 314).

Dale, Doris C. "Development of Classification Systems for Government Publications," *Library Resources and Technical Services* 13:471-483 (Fall 1969).

Free, Opal M. "Commercial Reprints of Federal Documents: Their Significance and Acquisition," *Special Libraries* 51:126-131 (March 1969).

Hiss, Sophie. *A.L.A. Rules for Filing Catalog Cards.* Chicago, American Library Association, 1942.

Jackson, Ellen P. "Cataloging, Classification, and Storage in a Separate Documents Collection," *Library Trends* 15:50-57 (July 1966).

Jackson, Ellen P. *A Manual for the Administration of the Federal Documents Collection in Libraries.* Chicago, American Library Association, 1955.

Jackson, Ellen P. *A Notation for a Public Documents Classification.* (Oklahoma A.&M. College Bulletin, No. 8). Stillwater, Okla., Oklahoma A.&M. College, 1946.

Jackson, Isabel H. "Advantages and Disadvantages of a Subject System of Classification As Key to a Depository Collection," *College and Research Libraries* 12:42-45 (January 1951).

Markley, Anne E. *Library Records for Government Publications.* Berkeley, University of California Press, 1951.

Paulson, Peter J. "Government Documents and Other Non-Trade Publications," *Library Trends* 18:363-372 (January 1970).

Pease, Mina. "The Plain 'J': A Documents Classification System," *Library Resources and Technical Services* 16:315-325 (Summer 1972).

Piggott, Mary. "The Cataloguing of Government Publications," *Library Association Record* 58:129-135 (April 1956).

Poole, Mary Elizabeth. *Documents Office Classification to 1966.* 3rd ed. Ann Arbor, Mich., University Microfilms, Inc., 1967.

Poole, Mary Elizabeth, and Ella Frances Smith. *Documents Office Classification Numbers for Cuttered Documents 1910-1924.* Ann Arbor, Mich., University Microfilms, Inc., 1960.

Spalding, C. S. "LC Practice with Regard to U.S. Documents," *Library Resources and Technical Services* 14:609-610 (Fall 1970).

Shaw, Thomas Shuler. "Distribution and Acquisition: Federal, State and Local Government Publications," *Library Trends* 15:36-49 (July 1966).

Simmons, Robert M. "Handling Changes in Superintendent of Documents Classification," *Library Resources and Technical Services* 15:241-244 (Spring 1971).

U.S. Superintendent of Documents. *Author Headings for United States Public Documents As Used in the Official Catalogues of the Superintendent of Documents.* 3rd ed. Washington, GPO, 1915. (Bulletin 18).

Western Michigan University. Department of Librarianship. *A List of Headings for United States Government Bodies Determined According to the Anglo-American Cataloging Rules.* Kalamazoo, Mich., Western Michigan University, 1968.

APPENDIX A—TABLES OF CLASSIFICATION*

TABLE I—DEPARTMENT AND AGENCY
SYMBOLS CURRENTLY IN USE

A	Agriculture Department
AA	Action
AC	Arms Control and Disarmament Agency
C	Commerce Department
CC	Federal Communications Commission
CR	Civil Rights Commission
CS	Civil Service Commission
CZ	Panama Canal Company and Canal Zone Government
D	Defense Department
DC	District of Columbia
EP	Environmental Protection Agency
FA	Fine Arts Commission
FCA	Farm Credit Administration
FHL	Federal Home Loan Bank Board
FM	Federal Mediation and Conciliation Service
FMC	Federal Maritime Commission
FP	Federal Power Commission
FR	Federal Reserve System Board of Governors
FT	Federal Trade Commission
FTZ	Foreign Trade Zones Board
GA	General Accounting Office
GP	Government Printing Office
GS	General Services Administration
HE	Health, Education, and Welfare Department
HH	Housing and Urban Development Department
I	Interior Department
IA	United States Information Agency
IC	Interstate Commerce Commission
J	Justice Department
Ju	Judiciary (Courts of the United States)
L	Labor Department

*Tables I through III are current as of April 1974. They were originally a part of the 1970 edition of *An Explanation of the Superintendent of Documents Classification System* (Washington, Government Printing Office) and have been updated for this book.

LC   Library of Congress
LR   National Labor Relations Board
NA   National Academy of Sciences
NAS   National Aeronautics and Space Administration
NC   National Capital Planning Commission
NCU   National Credit Union Administration
NF   National Foundation on the Arts and the Humanities
NMB   National Mediation Board
NS   National Science Foundation
OP   Overseas Private Investment Corporation
P   Post Office Department
Pr   President of United States
PrEx   Executive Office of the President
RA   National Railroad Adjustment Board
RnB   Renegotiation Board
RR   Railroad Retirement Board
S   State Department
SBA   Small Business Administration
SE   Securities and Exchange Commission
SI   Smithsonian Institution
T   Treasury Department
TC   Tariff Commission
TD   Transportation Department
VA   Veterans Administration
X
and   Congress
Y

TABLE II–AGENCY SYMBOLS OF BOARDS, COMMISSIONS, AND COMMITTEES ESTABLISHED BY ACT OF CONGRESS OR UNDER AUTHORITY OF ACT OF CONGRESS (not specifically designated in the Executive Branch of the Government nor as completely independent agencies)

Y 3.Ad6:   Administrative Conference of United States
Y 3.Ad9/6:   Administrative Conference of United States
Y 3.Ad9/7:   Advisory Commission on Information
Y 3.Ad9/8:   Advisory Commission on Intergovernmental Relations
Y 3.Ad9/9:   Advisory Commission on International Education and Cultural Affairs
Y 3.Al 1s: Federal Field Committee for Development Planning in Alaska
Y 3.Am3:   American Battle Monuments Commission
Y 3.Ap4/2:   Appalachian Regional Commission
Y 3.At6:   Atlantic-Pacific Interoceanic Canal Study Commission
Y 3.At7:   Atomic Energy Commission
Y 3.Av5:   Aviation Advisory Commission
Y 3.B61:   Committee on Purchase of Blind-Made Products
Y 3.C49/2:   Civil War Centennial Commission

Y 3.C63/2:   Coastal Plains Regional Commission
Y 3.C66:   Coinage Joint Commission
Y 3.C76/3:   Consumer Product Safety Commission
Y 3.C86:   National Advisory Commission on Criminal Justice Standards and
               Goals
Y 3.D37/2:   Delaware River Basin Commission
Y 3.Ed8:   Federal Interagency Committee on Education
Y 3.Ed8/2:   National Advisory Council on Education of Disadvantaged Children
Y 3.Ed8/3:   National Advisory Council on Education Professions Development
Y 3.Em3/2:   Emergency Loan Guarantee Board
Y 3.Eq2:   Equal Employment Opportunity Commission
Y 3.Ex7/3:   Export-Import Bank of United States
Y 3.Ex8:   National Advisory Council on Extension and Continuing Education
Y 3.F31/8:   Federal Deposit Insurance Corporation
Y 3.F31/13:   Federal Inter-Agency River Basin Committee
Y 3.F31/14:   Federal Inter-Agency Committee on Recreation
Y 3.F31/16:   Federal Council for Science and Technology
Y 3.F31/17:   Federal Radiation Council
Y 3.F31/18:   Federal Committee on Pest Control
Y 3.F31/19:   Federal Committee on Research Natural Areas
Y 3.F31/20:   Federal Executive Board
Y 3.F51:   National Commission on Fire Prevention and Control
Y 3.F76/3:   Foreign Claims Settlement Commission
Y 3.F76/4:   Foreign Scholarship Board
Y 3.F82:   Four Corners Regional Commission
Y 3.G79/3:   Great Lakes Basin Commission
Y 3.H62:   Advisory Council on Historic Preservation
Y 3.H73:   Permanent Committee for the Oliver Wendell Holmes Devise
Y 3.In2/6:   Indian Claims Commission
Y 3.In2/8:   National Industrial Pollution Control Council
Y 3.In2/9:   National Council on Indian Opportunity
Y 3.In8/6:   Interdepartmental Committee on Children and Youth
Y 3.In8/8:   Inter-Agency Committee on Water Resources
Y 3.In8/13:   Interdepartmental Committee on Nutrition for National Defense
Y 3.In8/15:   Commission on International Rules of Judicial Procedure
Y 3.In8/16:   Interagency Committee on Automatic Data Processing
Y 3.In8/17:   Interdepartmental Committee to Coordinate Federal Urban Area
               Assistance Programs
Y 3.In8/21:   Interdepartmental Committee on Status of Women
Y 3.In8/23:   Interagency Committee on Mexican-American Affairs
Y 3.J66:   Joint Publications Research Service
Y 3.J98:   Interdepartmental Council to Coordinate All Federal Juvenile
               Delinquency Programs
Y 3.L22:   Interagency Land Acquisitions Conference
Y 3.L58:   Lewis and Clark Trail Commission
Y 3.M33:   Maritime Advisory Committee
Y 3.M33/2:   Marihuana and Drug Abuse Commission
Y 3.M41:   National Commission on Materials Policy
Y 3.M58:   Migratory Bird Conservation Commission

Y 3.M69:   Missouri Basin Inter-Agency Committee
Y 3.M69/2:   Missouri River Basin Commission
Y 3.M84:   Mortgage Interest Rates Commission
Y 3.N21/16:   National Advisory Council on International Monetary and Financial Problems
Y 3.N21/21:   National Capital Transportation Agency
Y 3.N21/22:   National Commission on Food Marketing
Y 3.N21/23:   National Visitors Center Study Commission
Y 3.N21/24:   National Water Commission
Y 3.N21/25:   National Commission on Product Safety
Y 3.N21/27:   National Business Council for Consumer Affairs
Y 3.N42/2:   New England Regional Commission
Y 3.N42/3:   New England River Basins Commission
Y 3.N81/3:   North Atlantic Regional Water Resources Study Coordinating Committee
Y 3.Ob7:   Obscenity and Pornography Commission
Y 3.Oc1:   Occupational Safety and Health Review Commission
Y 3.Oc2:   National Advisory Committee on Oceans and Atmosphere
Y 3.Oz1:   Ozarks Regional Commission
Y 3.P11/2:   Pacific Southwest Inter-agency Committee
Y 3.P11/4:   Pacific Northwest River Basins Commission
Y 3.P81:   Population Growth and the American Future, Commission on
Y 3.P84/4:   Postal Rate Commission
Y 3.P93/4:   Price Commission
Y 3.P96/7:   Public Land Law Review Commission
Y 3.P97:   Purchase of Products and Services of the Blind and Other Severely Handicapped Committee
Y 3.R11:   Interagency Racial Data Committee
Y 3.R13/3:   Railroad Retirement Commission
Y 3.R67:   Franklin Delano Roosevelt Memorial Commission
Y 3.Se4:   Selective Service System
Y 3.Sh6:   Ship Structure Committee
Y 3.Sh6/2:   American Shipbuilding Commission
Y 3.So8:   Souris-Red-Rainy River Basin Commission
Y 3.Sp2/7:   Cabinet Committee on Opportunity for Spanish Speaking People
Y 3.St8:   Strategy Council on Drug Abuse
Y 3.Su1:   Subversive Activities Control Board
Y 3.T22:   National Commission on Technology, Automation, and Economic Progress
Y 3.T25:   Tennessee Valley Authority
Y 3.T64:   National Tourism Resources Review Commission
Y 3.Up6:   Upper Great Lakes Regional Commission
Y 3.V85:   National Advisory Council on Vocational Education
Y 3.W29:   Water Resources Council
Y 3.W58:   White House Conferences
Y 3.W89/3:   National Commission on State Workmen's Compensation Laws

TABLE III—AGENCY SYMBOLS OF CURRENT
CONGRESSIONAL COMMITTEES (Temporary select
and special committees not included)

Y 4.Ae8:	Aeronautical and Space Sciences (Senate)
Y 4.Ag4:	Special Committee on Aging (Senate)
Y 4.Ag8/1:	Agriculture (House)
Y 4.Ag8/2:	Agriculture and Forestry (Senate)
Y 4.Ap6/1:	Appropriations (House)
Y 4.Ap6/2:	Appropriations (Senate)
Y 4.Ar5/2:	Armed Services (House)
Y 4.Ar5/3:	Armed Services (Senate)
Y 4.At7/2:	Joint Committee on Atomic Energy
Y 4.B22/1:	Banking and Currency (House)
Y 4.B22/3:	Banking and Currency (Senate)
Y 4.C73/2:	Commerce (Senate)
Y 4.C76/7:	Congressional Operations Joint Committee
Y 4.D36:	Joint Committee on Defense Production
Y 4.D63/1:	District of Columbia (House)
Y 4.D63/2:	District of Columbia (Senate)
Y 4.Ec7:	Joint Economic Committee
Y 4.Ed8/1:	Education and Labor (House)
Y 4.F49:	Finance (Senate)
Y 4.F76/1:	Foreign Affairs (House)
Y 4.F76/2:	Foreign Relations (Senate)
Y 4.G74/6:	Government Operations (Senate)
Y 4.G74/7:	Government Operations (House)
Y 4.H81/3:	House Administration (House)
Y 4.In8/4:	Interstate and Foreign Commerce (House)
Y 4.In8/11:	Joint Committee on Internal Revenue Taxation
Y 4.In8/13:	Interior and Insular Affairs (Senate)
Y 4.In8/14:	Interior and Insular Affairs (House)
Y 4.In8/15:	Internal Security Committee (House)
Y 4.J89/1:	Judiciary (House)
Y 4.J89/2:	Judiciary (Senate)
Y 4.L11/2:	Labor and Public Welfare (Senate)
Y 4.L61/2:	Joint Committee on the Library
Y 4.M53:	Merchant Marine and Fisheries (House)
Y 4.N22/4:	Joint Committee on Navajo-Hopi Indian Administration
Y 4.P84/10:	Post Office and Civil Service (House)
Y 4.P84/11:	Post Office and Civil Service (Senate)
Y 4.P93/1:	Joint Committee on Printing
Y 4.P96/10:	Public Works (Senate)
Y 4.P96/11:	Public Works (House)
Y 4.R24/4:	Joint Committee on Reduction of Federal Expenditures
Y 4.R86/1:	Rules (House)
Y 4.R86/2:	Rules and Administration (Senate)
Y 4.Sci2:	Science and Astronautics (House)
Y 4.Sm1:	Small Business Select Committee (House)

Y 4.Sm1/2:	Small Business Select Committee (Senate)
Y 4.St2/3:	Standards of Official Conduct (House)
Y 4.V64/3:	Veterans' Affairs (House)
Y 4.V64/4:	Veterans' Affairs Committee (Senate)
Y 4.W36:	Ways and Means (House)

APPENDIX B—FLOW CHART

This chart was made by Mary Sue Ferrell, University of Kentucky, College of Library Science, Intern.

Processing of Depository Shipment

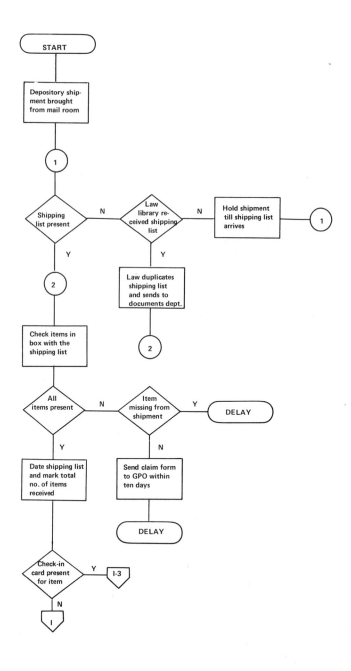

Processing of Depository Shipment (cont'd)

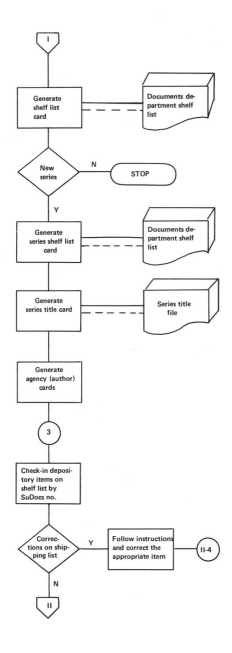

Processing of Depository Shipment (cont'd)

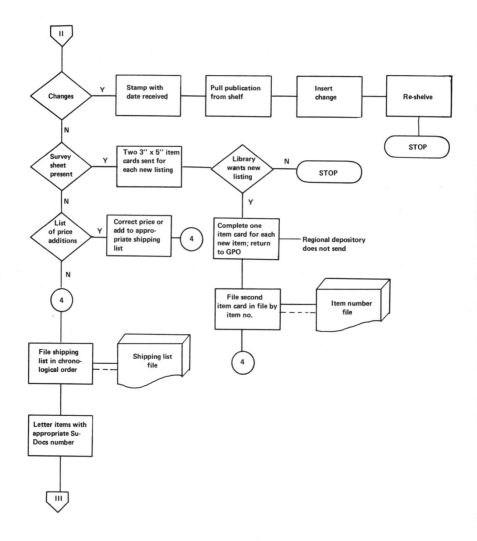

Processing of Depository Shipment (cont'd)

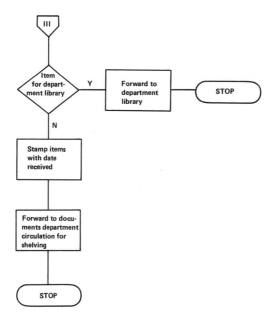

Request for Item on Depository Account

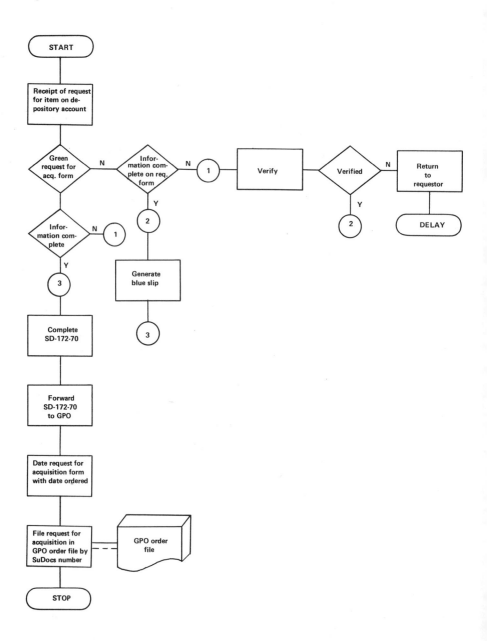

Receipt of Item Requested on Depository Account

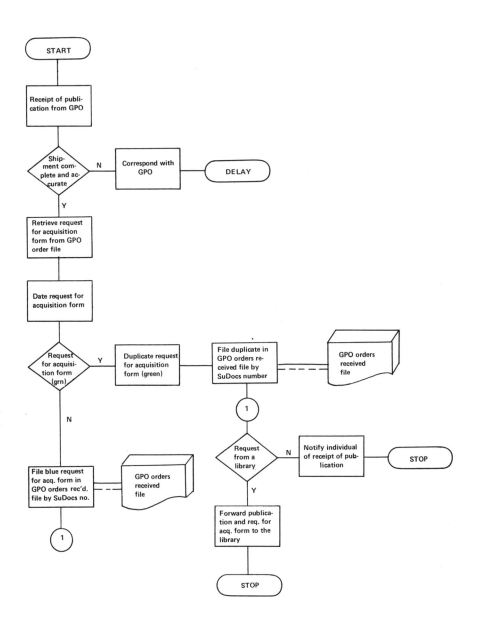

Claim of Depository Items

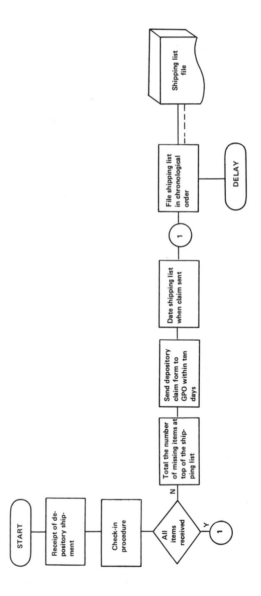

Receipt of Claimed Depository Items

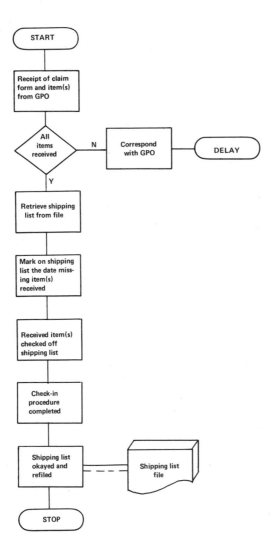

Cataloging Process for Government Publications

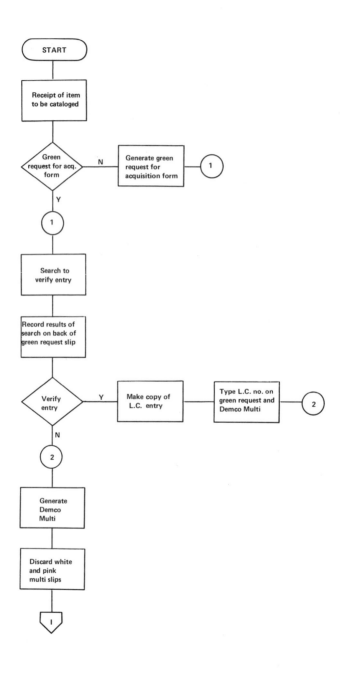

Cataloging Process for Government Publications (cont'd)

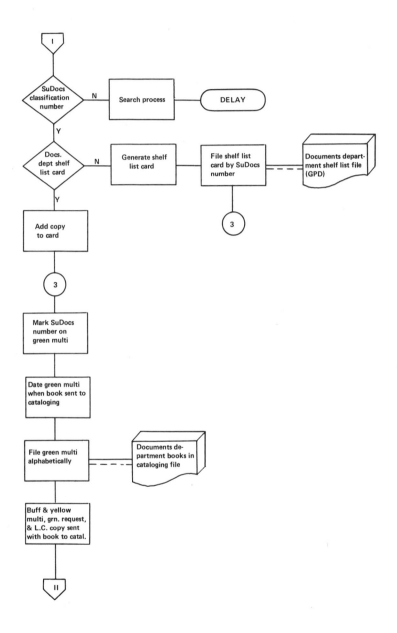

Cataloging Process for Government Publications (cont'd)

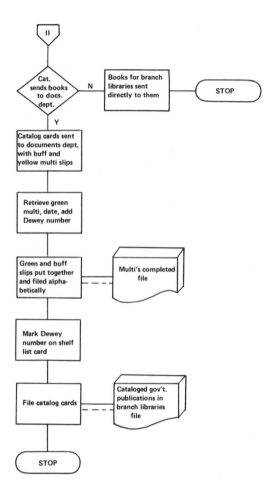

APPENDIX C–SHIPPING LISTS

LIBRARY,
PUBLIC DOCUMENTS DEPARTMENT,
U.S. GOVERNMENT PRINTING OFFICE,
WASHINGTON, D.C. 20402

DAILY DEPOSITORY
SHIPPING LIST

5.21.74

Claims for nonreceipt of publications on this list under item numbers previously selected by a library must be postmarked within ten days of the date of receiving it. (Instructions to Depository Libraries, Revised September 1967, page 9.)	Shipping List __7307__
	Shipment of
	May 6, 1974

Item No.		Class
250-E-2	The NOAA Story	C 55.2:N21oc/2
288-A	Hearing Before the USCCR, Held in Cairo, Ill., Mar. 23-25,1972 *$4.25 S/N 0500-00091	CR 1.8:C 12
299	Pam 78, The Federal Manager's Responsibilities under the Merit System, Feb.1974 *30c S/N 0600-00774	CS 1.48:78
314-A	INTERIM FIIG T277(Reprint) Vehicles & Trailers, Apr.25,1974 *	D 7.6/4:V 53/rep.
508-H-3	Current Bibliography of Epidemiology Vol.6, No.5, May 1974 *$2.25	HE 20.3617:6/5
610-A	Current Fisheries Statistics No.	C 55.309/2:
	6118, South Carolina Landings, Annual Summary 1972	
	6398, Frozen Fishery Products, Jan.1974	
	6429, New York Landings, Jan. 1974	
	6449, New York Landings, Feb.1974	
619-D	Journal of Research of the Geological Survey Vol.2, No.2, Mar.-Apr.1974 *$2.75	I 19.61:2/2
831-C-2	A Bibliography of Drug Abuse Literature, 1972 *$2.55 Note: New class added to this Item No. (title of publication is series)	HE 20.8211:D84/972
936	Light List Vol.1, Atlantic Coast, St.Croix River, Maine to Little River, South Carolina, 1974, CG-158 *$4.75 S/N 5012-00073	TD 5.9:v.1/974
1017	Hearings: Trade Preferences: Latin America & the Caribbean	Y 4.F 76/1:L 34/8
1021	Hearings: Energy Transportation Security Act of 1974, Serial No.93-26	Y 4.M 53:93-26
1022	Hearings: Operation & Organization of the Postal Rate Commission, Serial No. 93-43	Y 4.P 84/10:93-43
1033	Hearings: Vehicle Use in the Federal Government, FY 1974	Y4.Ap 6/2:V 53/974

* For Sale by the Superintendent of Documents

LIST OF PRICE ADDITIONS AND
CLASS CORRECTIONS

Shipping List 7193, January 17, 1974

486-F   Dental Services for American Indians and Alaska Natives, fy 1973
Note: Change class from HE 20.*2659*:973 to HE 20.*5309*:973.
This is a change in class due to the reorganization of the Public Health Service.

Shipping List 7251, 2nd Shipment, March 15, 1974

486-I-2   Preparation for Health Career Advancement for American Indians, etc.
Note: Change in class from HE 20.*2652*:H34/4 to HE 20.*5302*: H34/4.
This is a change due to the reorganization of the Public Health Service.

Shipping List 7256, 1st Shipment, March 20, 1974

461 (Rev.   Personnel Evaluation in Vocational and Technical Education,
1965)   Infor.Ser. No.99. Change class from HE *5.2:P43/4* to HE *18.11/2:99*.
Student Evaluation in Vocational and Technical Education, Infor. Ser. No.97. Change class from HE *5.2:St9/5* to HE *18.11/2:97* and change Item No. on both to read Item No. 461-D-2.

INDEX

Author and title entries in this index refer to works discussed in the text.

DATE DUE